The Way to Win

by
William Le Queux

The Way to Win
by William Le Queux

Copyright © 2023

All Rights reserved.

No part of this publication may be reproduced, stored in a retrieval system, or transmitted in any form or by any means, electronic, mechanical, photocopying or Otherwise, without the written permission of the publisher.
The author/editor asserts the moral right to be identified as the author/editor of this work.

ISBN: 978-93-59950-65-5

Published by
DOUBLE 9 BOOKS
2/13-B, Ansari Road
Daryaganj, New Delhi – 110002
info@double9books.com
www.double9books.com
Tel. 011-40042856

This book is under public domain

ABOUT THE AUTHOR

Anglo-French journalist and author William Tufnell Le Queux was born on July 2, 1864, and died on October 13, 1927. He was also a diplomat (honorary consul for San Marino), a traveler (in Europe, the Balkans, and North Africa), a fan of flying (he presided over the first British air meeting at Doncaster in 1909), and a wireless pioneer who played music on his own station long before radio was widely available. However, he often exaggerated his own skills and accomplishments. The Great War in England in 1897 (1894), a fantasy about an invasion by France and Russia, and The Invasion of 1910 (1906), a fantasy about an invasion by Germany, are his best-known works. Le Queux was born in the city. The man who raised him was English, and his father was French. He went to school in Europe and learned art in Paris from Ignazio (or Ignace) Spiridon. As a young man, he walked across Europe and then made a living by writing for French newspapers. He moved back to London in the late 1880s and managed the magazines Gossip and Piccadilly. In 1891, he became a parliamentary reporter for The Globe. He stopped working as a reporter in 1893 to focus on writing and traveling.

CONTENTS

Chapter One
The Rift in the Clouds...7

Chapter Two
Our Invincible Navy..17

Chapter Three
The Coming Victory on Land...27

Chapter Four
Our Mastery of the Air..37

Chapter Five
Britain's Unshakable Resolve...47

Chapter Six
The Terror in Germany...54

Chapter Seven
Germany's Bankrupt Future...63

Chapter Eight
The Invisible Hand..72

Chapter Nine
Compulsory Service Britain's Master-Stroke 82

Chapter Ten
Germany's Colossal Blunders 91

Chapter Eleven
Victory with Honour 102

Chapter Twelve
"Never Again"..111

Chapter One
The Rift in the Clouds

If we could imagine a being from another planet dropped suddenly on this old earth of ours and left with the aid of maps to figure out for himself the real position of the world-war, we could readily imagine that it would seem to him that the Germans were winning "hands down."

Perhaps there would be a good deal of excuse for such a belief.

He would see, in the first place, that the Germans had overrun and captured the whole of Belgium except one very small portion. He would see that the greater part of Northern France was in their undisputed possession. He would see that they had driven the Russians from Poland and penetrated far within the boundaries of Russia proper.

He would also see that they had almost completely conquered or cajoled the Balkan States, and that German trains were running from the North Sea to Constantinople. He would see them holding apparently impregnable lines of defences against forces at least as strong as their own—probably much stronger. He would see them or their Allies holding up British forces in Persia and in Mesopotamia. He would see the Italians apparently firmly held along the mountainous boundaries of the Austrian Empire. He would see that a great British army had been driven out of Gallipoli. He would unquestionably come to the conclusion that the cause of the Allies was a lost cause, and would probably conclude that the best thing they could do would be to make a speedy peace on the best terms the victors could be induced to grant.

And he would be unquestionably wrong in his deduction, even though we admit the accuracy of his facts.

For, like the thoughtless and the whimperers among us, he would for want of knowledge leave out of his consideration certain hard facts which, properly considered, would reverse his judgment. Like the thoughtless and the whimperers, he would judge too much from mere appearances and would fail to see the real essential things. He would fail to see the wood for the trees; he would mistake the shadow for the substance. Just so the German people to-day are making the mistake of thinking that the occupation of enemy territory, a mere temporary advantage gained through treacherous preparation for war at a time when they professed to be working for peace, constitutes the victory that must be theirs before they could hope to gain the world-dominion upon which, as we now know, their hearts and the hearts of their rulers have been set for the last forty years.

For eighteen months the civilised world has been struggling against the most formidable menace to its liberties by which it has ever been faced. For eighteen months we have seen the enemy apparently going on from triumph to triumph. We have seen the devastation of Belgium, the crucifixion of a little people whose only wish was that they should be allowed to live their happy lives in peace, and whose only crime was that they dared to resist the Prussian bully. We have seen the martyrdom of Poland. We have seen the very heart of France—incomparable Paris—threatened with destruction.

We have seen the stately memorials of a great civilisation, such as Germany has never known and never can know, wrecked and plundered. We have seen innocent civilians murdered in hundreds, women and children sent to death or a far worse fate. We have seen the ruin of Serbia. We have lost thousands of our best and bravest sons. We have seen the tragic failure in the Gallipoli Peninsula—itself a mere incident of the world-war, yet one of the greatest military undertakings upon which we have ever embarked. We have failed conspicuously to protect the little nations in whose cause we drew the sword, and who have gone down in ruin under the iron heel of a ferocious tyranny beside which the worst oppression of historic times seems mild in comparison. Can it be a matter of wonder if the cry, "How long, O Lord, how long?" goes up from the fainting heart of outraged civilisation?

Yet the darkest hour is ever the herald of the dawn; and if to-day we try with a single mind to penetrate the fog and mystery with which this greatest of all wars is surrounded, we shall see that there is really and truly a rift in the clouds. No doubt we have still many days of storm and stress before us. The end is not yet. But, in the noble language of the King, the goal is drawing into sight. The sun of victory is not yet shining fully upon us, but none the less the dawn is at hand. Already its first faint gleams are breaking in upon our eyes; there are abundant signs, if we lift up our hearts and our courage, that the long period of gloom and depression is passing away.

Properly to understand the position as it exists to-day we must look backward to the years 1870 and 1871, for in those years was born the spirit of aggression and arrogance which ever since has been the driving power of Germany. After years of preparation, when so far as possible everything was ready, Germany fell suddenly upon a France torn by internal dissensions, weak through want of preparation, and utterly unready for war. Naturally there could be but one end to such a conflict, and a few short months saw France helpless beneath the heel of the invader. Germany emerged from that war with almost incalculable profit, firmly imbued with the idea that she was invincible, and convinced that at any moment she chose she could reach out her greedy hands and grasp the sceptre of European domination. Then, as she thought, she could with safety enter upon a conflict with an England which had grown over-rich and perhaps over-lazy. Then the real enemy could be crushed, and the world-dominion of which her megalomaniac rulers dreamed would be within her grasp.

If a nation has determined upon war, there is never any lack of excuse, and Germany chose her time well. Her blow fell at a time when no single one of the Allies was prepared for war. That fact alone fixes absolutely the responsibility for the present appalling conflict, and in the days to come the unanimous verdict of history will be that the War was deliberately provoked by Germany through sheer greed and lust of power.

For, be it remembered, there was no legitimate ambition before Germany which she was not perfectly free to enjoy. Her trade was free and unhampered, the seas were as open to her use as to our own, she possessed vast colonial dominions which gave her every opportunity for all the legitimate expansion of which she could dream for centuries to come. She had grown rich and prosperous in the exercise of the freedom which she has ever been the first to deny to others. No one menaced her or sought to do her injury. But she was the *nouveau riche* among the nations. She had been poisoned for a long course of years with the false doctrine that the German was something essentially superior to the peoples of other races, and she owes her approaching downfall, which is as certain as the rising of to-morrow's sun, to the blind teachers of the blind who have imbued her with that spirit of envy and arrogance which may be as fatal to a nation as to an individual.

We all know only too well what happened when war broke out. Germany, with her armies trained to the hour after years of patient preparation, with her forces ready to the last man and the last gun, shamelessly broke her plighted word with the invasion of Belgium. She had counted that there, at least, she would meet with no resistance; she could not realise that a little people, even to save its honour, would dare to oppose the onrush of her countless hordes. In that she made her first and, perhaps, her greatest mistake. Just as she thought that England would not draw the sword for a "scrap of paper," so she thought that Belgium would not dare to resist.

We know now that she was wrong; we know, too, that the heroism of the Belgians surely saved Europe in those first days by gaining the priceless time which enabled France and England to throw their scanty forces across the path of the invader, which led ultimately to the great battle of the Marne, that titanic conflict which surely and decisively smashed once and for ever the German plans. In spite of all that has happened since, in spite of the apparent victories Germany has won, in spite of the territories she has occupied, the defeat of the Marne marked the beginning of her final overthrow.

But the peril was appalling. France, Russia, and Britain were alike unprepared for war, short of men, short of munitions, short of everything which would have enabled them at once to meet the common enemy on anything like equal terms. The days are gone for ever when victory can be won by men alone; modern war is too machine-like in its developments, the importance of supplies and organisation is far too great to give a poorly equipped army the slightest chance of success. Not men alone, but munitions are the secret of success to-day, and every single advantage that Germany has won since war broke out has been won by her superiority in mechanical equipment. Her men, considered individually, are certainly not the equals of either the French or the Russians or the British; they have neither the dash of the French, nor the dogged courage and endurance of the Russians, nor the personal *sang-froid* and cool initiative of the British. But Germany had the numbers and the equipment, and to numbers and equipment alone she owes such successes as she has gained.

Caught unprepared at the outset of war, the Allies were naturally in a position which must well have seemed hopeless. Germany reaped to the full the advantages which she had sought in long preparation for war under the guise of peace. Her armies plunged forward with resistless momentum until they were within sight of the very gates of Paris, and in the eyes of the world it was merely a matter of time as to when she would occupy the French capital. Then came Von Kluck's amazing blunder, the swift stroke of the French and British against the German right wing, and the precipitate retreat which led to the defeat at the Marne. From that day, in spite of apparent successes, the fortunes of Germany have been on the wane.

There was no mistake about the reply of civilisation to the German menace. France, Russia, and England threw down the guage in the most unmistakable terms in the historic declaration that neither would conclude a separate peace without the others. That, we have now to recognise, is one of the main facts which must operate most powerfully in bringing about the final defeat of Germany. In no particular can she hope to rival the resources of the Allies, and so long as the Allies hang together they are unmistakably on the road to final victory. It is for this reason that at the present moment it is the main object of German diplomacy to sow distrust and suspicion among the partners in the Quadruple Entente. Their one and only hope—and they know it—is to provoke a quarrel among the Allies which would not merely rob the Allies of all hope of final victory, but would give the Huns and their dupes a reasonable chance—indeed, more than a reasonable chance—of snatching triumph from the very jaws of defeat.

There is a school of croakers very much in evidence in England at present who can see nothing of good in anything which their own country has done and is doing. They remind one of Gilbert's

> Idiot who praises in enthusiastic tone
> Each century but this, and every country but his own.

They are, of course, always with us, but at the present moment they are more than usually aggressive, and we notice them perhaps more than is good for us. They are the chief source of that dangerous form of pessimism which we see exemplifying itself in a constant belittling of the enormous efforts and the enormous sacrifices which this country has made. According to these mischievous propagandists, nothing we do or have done can possibly be sufficient or right. The effects of this perpetual "calamity howling" on our own people is bad enough; it is far worse upon the peoples of the Allied countries and the neutrals, because, not understanding our national peculiarities, they are apt to take us at a wholly absurd valuation and to think that, as our own people are constantly accusing us of slackness in a war in which we have so much at stake, there must be something in the charge. If plenty of mud is thrown, some of it is tolerably sure to stick, and there can be no doubt that the perpetual depreciation of British efforts by people in this country has had a most dangerous effect, and has, in fact, played the German game to perfection both here and abroad.

Those who wish to form an adequate realisation of what Britain has really done in the cause of civilisation should try to take a longer view, and try also to throw their minds backward to the condition of affairs which existed when the declaration of war came eighteen months ago. They should try, in fact, to learn something of the lessons taught by our past history.

We can start with the indisputable and undisputed fact that so far as the war on land was concerned this country was entirely unprepared to take up the rôle it has since assumed. That is a proposition which not even the Germans, who are so ready to accuse England of having caused the War, can very well dispute. Throughout our history we have been a naval and not a military Power, though it is of course true that, judged by the standards of other days, we have now and again put forward very considerable military efforts.

But it was many a long year since British troops had fought on the Continent of Europe, and it is safe to assume that the great majority of people in this country, had they been asked, would have replied without hesitation that we should never again take part in the land fighting in a continental war.

Now it must be obvious to anyone who takes the trouble to give the matter a moment's thought that, for the purposes of war as it is understood by the great military nations of Europe, the British Army as it existed in August, 1914, was hopelessly inadequate. Our real strength lay on the sea, where it has always lain. It is true that, for its size, the British force which was thrown into Flanders in the early days of the struggle was perhaps the most perfectly trained and equipped army that ever took the field.

But no one will contend that it was adequate in size, and we know that the Germans regarded it as a "contemptible little army" that was to be brushed aside with hardly an effort by the German hordes. It consisted of perhaps 120,000 men, and undoubtedly, as our French friends have generously admitted, it played a part worthy of "the best and highest traditions" of our race. But it was not an army on the continental scale.

What has been done since? How have we taken up the task of creating forces which might be regarded as commensurate to meet the menace by which civilisation found itself faced?

Our "contemptible little army," thanks to the genius of Lord Kitchener, has grown until to-day it numbers something in the neighbourhood of four million men. That is a fact which the world knows and recognises, and in itself alone it is sufficient to refute the contention of those who are to be found preaching in and out of season that Britain's efforts have been lamentably inadequate. Great armies are not to be made in a day or a year, they do not spring fully armed from the earth, and the fact that we, a naval rather than a military Power, have in the course of eighteen months raised and equipped forces on such a scale ought to be sufficient to confound those shallow critics who are eternally bewailing our supposed "slackness," which, as a matter of fact, has no existence outside their own disordered imaginations. I do not believe there is to be found to-day a military writer whose opinion is of any value who would not agree that the effort which Britain has made is one of the most stupendous in all military history.

In France, in Russia, and in Italy everyone whose authority is regarded as having any substantial basis is agreed on the point, and the Germans themselves, however they may affect to sneer at our army of "hirelings," know a great deal too much about military matters not to recognise that one of the very gravest of their perils is the growing military power of England. That power will be exercised to the full when the time comes, and it will assuredly be found to be of the very greatest importance in bringing about the overthrow of German hopes and ambitions.

We all know—the whole world knows—why the military power of England has not yet reached its full majesty. We all know that in the War of to-day a superabundance of munitions is demanded which none could have expected from the history of the past. Every form of military stores—guns, rifles, shell, ammunition—all must be provided on a scale of colossal magnitude.

It is the fact that Germany alone of all the warring nations partly realised this, and in her careful preparations for a war of her own seeking, for which she chose her own time, accumulated in the days of peace such enormous reserves of munitions as she hoped would render her to a large extent independent of manufacture during the actual period of fighting. It is certain that Germany hoped to overthrow Russia and France in a series of swift, brief attacks without trenching dangerously upon her reserve stocks. We know now that she was wrong; but we know, too, that she came within an ace of success.

That she realised her error and embarked upon the manufacture of munitions on a vast scale is true, but none the less it is also true that she cannot hope to compete in this respect with the united resources of the Allies once they get into their full stride. Slowly, perhaps, but none the less surely, she is being overtaken even in the department which she made almost exclusively her own, and the day is coming when she will have not the remotest prospect of keeping up an adequate reply to the storm of high explosives which will break upon her lines east, west, north, and south. When that day comes—and it may be nearer than most of us think—we shall see the swiftest of changes in the present position of the War. There will be an end at last to the long deadlock in which we and our Allies have been forced to act on the defensive.

Already, indeed, the change is in sight. Germany to-day, in spite of her frantic struggles, is absolutely and firmly held in a ring of steel. She is, in every real sense of the word, on the defensive; her spasmodic attacks are purely defensive in their origin and conception, and the steadily increasing pressure of her foes must sooner or later find and break through some weak spot in lines which are already seriously extended and must soon wear thin.

I do not pretend for a moment that everything has gone as well as we could wish; I do not pretend that there have not been mistakes, delays, lack of decision, lack of foresight. No war was ever fought without mistakes; we are not a race of supermen. But I do say that we have made such an effort as has perhaps never been made in history before to meet a series of conditions of which neither we in particular nor the world at large has ever experienced.

The nation that could wage war without making mistakes would very speedily dominate the world.

If the Germans had not made mistakes at least as great as those of the Allies, they would long ago have won a supreme and crushing victory which would have left the whole of Europe prostrate at their feet. Whereas what do we see to-day? The plain, unalterable fact is that in her sudden assault upon nations wholly unprepared for it Germany has not won a single success of the nature which is decisive. She did not succeed in "knocking out" either of the enemies who really count, and she soon found herself condemned to a long and dragging war of the very nature which all her experts, for years past, have admitted must be fatal to German hopes and ambitions. Germany has always postulated for success swift and shattering blows; she believed she could deal such blows at her enemies in detail before she was defeated by a prepared unity against which she must be powerless. She hoped to shatter France before the slow-moving Russians could get into their stride, and leave her ruined and crushed while she turned to meet the menace from the East. She counted on winning the hegemony of Europe before she could be checked by a combination ready to meet her on more than level terms. There she made the first and greatest of her mistakes, a mistake from the effects of which she can never recover.

And will anyone contend that, in bringing the German design to hopeless ruin, Britain has not played a worthy part? Will anyone be found bold enough to assert that the position on the Continent to-day would not have been very widely different if Britain had chosen the ignoble part and refused to unsheath the sword in defence of those great principles for which our forefathers in all ages have been ready to fight and to die? Will anyone venture to express a doubt that, but for the assistance of Britain, France must have been crushed? And, with France helpless and Britain neutral, what would have been Russia's chance of escaping disaster?

I need hardly say that I do not put these suggestions forward with any idea of belittling the part—the very great and very heroic part—which has been played in the great world-tragedy by France and Russia. But I do seriously suggest—and French and Russian writers have been the first generously to admit it—that England's assistance has made their campaigns possible.

If we have not done the terrific fighting which has been done by France and Russia, we have at least borne a very respectable share in the fray; we can leave others to speak for us on this score. But we have supported our Allies in other fields; we have, to a very large extent, found the sinews of war; we have made of our land the workshop of the Allies, and poured out a stream of munitions which has been of the utmost value, even if it has not made all the difference between victory and defeat. And, above all and beyond all, we have, by our sea power, practically carried the campaigns of our Allies on our backs. Thanks to our unchallenged supremacy afloat, the Allies have been able to move in all parts of the world with a security unknown in any other war in history. While the German Fleet skulks in the fastnesses of the Kiel Canal, and the German flag has disappeared from the ocean highways of the world, the ships of the Allies move almost unhindered on their daily business, the endless supplies of men and munitions go to and fro unchallenged except by the lurking submarines of the enemy, which, for all their boastings, are powerless to affect vitally the ultimate issue or to do more than inflict damage which, compared with the targets offered them, is practically of no significance.

Has our country anything to be ashamed of in the contribution it has thus made to the war for the liberation of civilisation from the domination of brute force? Assuredly not. And when in the fullness of time the opportunity is offered us for a more striking demonstration of what British world-power means, I am confident that we shall see ample proof that the spirit and temper of our race is as fine as ever, and that we shall play a worthy part in the final overthrow of the common enemy. In the meantime let us make an end of the constant stream of self-depreciation which is far removed from real modesty and self-respect; let us do our part in that stern and silent temper which has for all time been part of our great heritage.

Stern work lies before us; the long-drawn agony is not yet even approaching its close. But we can best help forward the end if we approach our task not with empty boasting, not with perpetual whimperings and self-reproach, but with the cool courage and dogged determination which have carried us so far through the worst dangers that have threatened us in the past, and which, if we play our part without faltering, will yet bring us to a triumphant issue from the perils which beset us to-day.

Chapter Two
Our Invincible Navy

It is the brightest and most encouraging feature of the War that British supremacy at sea is unchallenged and probably unchallengeable by Germany.

It is true that the main German Fleet has not yet dared to give battle in the open sea, and that the endeavours of scattered units afloat have met with speedy disaster. It is no less true that should the "High Canal Admiral" venture forth from the secluded shelters in which the Imperial German Navy has for so many months concealed itself, its prospects of dealing a successful blow at the maritime might of Britain are exceedingly slender.

None the less, it is incredible that, sooner or later, the German Navy will fail to attempt what German writers are fond of describing as a "Hussar Stroke." We can contemplate that issue—and we know our sailors do so—with every confidence. In every single particular—in ships, in men, in moral, and in traditions—the British Navy is superior to that of Germany. Even without the powerful help we should receive from our French and Italian Allies, British control over the ocean highways is supreme.

A Radical journal, which for years past has been conspicuous for its laudation of everything German, has lately tried to make our flesh creep with tales of the mounting in German warships of a monster gun—said to be of 17-inch calibre—which was so utterly to outrange anything we possess as to render our control of the North Sea doubtful and shadowy.

It is strange to find a journal which, before the War, was one of the chief asserters of the peaceful intentions of Germany thus passing into the ranks of the "scaremongers." When the late Lord Roberts ventured, before the War, to point out the dangers which lay before us, he was denounced as an "alarmist." Yet on the very doubtful supposition that a single shell which fell into Dunkirk was a 17-inch missile the *Daily News* has built up a "scare" article worthy only of a race of panic-mongers, and full of false premises and false deductions from the first line to the last. Such are the changed views brought about by changed circumstances!

But even supposing that the Germans actually possess a 17-inch naval gun, is the *Daily News* content to assume that the Admiralty and the Government are not fully aware of the fact and that they have taken no steps whatever to meet the new danger? It is a literal fact that we have always been an inch or two ahead of Germany in the calibre of our biggest guns—the history of the Dreadnought fully proves that—and it is incredible that we should suddenly be caught napping in a matter on which we have led the world. I leave out of consideration the purely technical question as to whether such guns could by any possibility be fitted to ships designed and partly constructed to take smaller weapons; experts say that such a change would be impossible without what would amount to practical reconstruction.

Putting these considerations on one side, is the record of our naval service such as to justify us in assuming that they know less than they have always known of the plans and intentions of the enemy?

Mr Balfour's reply on the subject was plain and categorical; the naval authorities know nothing of any such weapon, and do not believe that it exists. In all probability we shall be quite safe in accepting their estimate of the situation, and whatever the facts may be the Navy may be trusted to deal with new perils as they arise. After all, a Navy is not merely so many ships and so many men armed with so many guns of such and such a size. That is a fact which, however imperfectly it is appreciated in Germany, is well known here. Tradition and moral count even more afloat than ashore; we possess both. A Navy whose chief achievements have been the drowning of helpless non-combatants in the infamous submarine campaign may hardly be said to possess either.

For many months now the German flag has vanished from the ocean highways of the world. For many months British commerce has peacefully pursued its pathways to the uttermost ends of the earth.

There have been times when the depredations of German raiders, such as the "Emden," caused some inconvenience and considerable loss. There have been times when the submarine campaign has apparently had a great measure of success. But though many ships, with their cargoes and with many innocent lives, have been sunk, nothing which the German pirates could do was sufficient seriously to threaten our overseas trade. Very soon the marauders were rounded up and destroyed, and in a space of time which, before the War, would have been deemed incredible the seas were practically free for the passage of the ships of the Allies.

In the early days of the War many good judges believed that the German commerce raiders would have been as effective against our overseas trade as were the French privateers in the days of the Napoleonic wars. Certain it is that it was the universal expectation that our losses in mercantile tonnage would have been far more grievous than has proved to be the case.

We see now that this expectation was unduly alarmist. But it was entertained not merely by amateur students of war, but by many of the sailors who have given a lifetime of thought to the problems of warfare at sea. Every lesson that could be drawn from history suggested that the life of the German raiders would have been far longer than actually proved to be the case. Those lessons, however, were learned in the days when the war fleets were composed of great sailing vessels which could keep the sea far longer without fresh supplies than is possible to-day. Cut off from any possible sources of regular supplies of food, coal, and ammunition, the few German ships which remained at liberty when war broke out were quickly hunted down by superior forces and destroyed until, a very few months after the outbreak of war, Germany's strength afloat was closely confined to the Baltic and a very small portion of the North Sea.

Nothing like the achievements of the British Navy has ever been witnessed in the history of war. Not even the most enthusiastic believer in sea power could have dreamed of such brilliant and striking successes; not even the most enthusiastic admirer of the British Navy could, in his most sanguine moments, have expected such results as have been attained.

When we come to think of the expanse of ocean to be covered, the services which the British Navy has rendered to civilisation will be seen to be stupendous. Not merely have all the German ships which were at liberty outside the North Sea and the Baltic been hunted down and destroyed, but the Grand Fleet, the darling of the Kaiser's heart, the object upon which millions have been poured out like water with the express purpose of crushing Britain, has been penned up in the narrowest of quarters, and from every strategical point of view has been reduced to practical impotence. True, it succeeded, under cover of fog and darkness, in sending a squadron of fast ships to bombard undefended Scarborough, where its gallant efforts resulted in the killing and wounding of some hundreds of women, children, and other non-combatants who, had we been fighting a civilised foe, would have been perfectly safe from harm. But a repetition of the attempt at this dastardly crime led to such condign punishment that the effort has never been repeated, and from that day to this German excursions at sea, so far, at least, as British waters are concerned, have been confined to the occasional appearance of stray torpedo craft and the campaign of submarine piracy and murder which has left upon the name of the German Navy a stigma which it will take centuries to eradicate.

With the one solitary exception of the unequal fight off Coronel, where the "Good Hope" and "Monmouth" were destroyed by the greatly superior squadron of Von Spee, the Germans have uniformly had the worse of any sea fighting which they ventured to undertake. Even the Baltic, in which they fondly imagined they had undisputed supremacy, has been rendered more than "unhealthy" by the activities of British submarines—so unhealthy, in fact, that the German attack upon the Gulf of Riga, which was to have led to the crushing of the Russian right wing and the advance upon Petrograd, ended in a dismal failure and the precipitate flight of the attackers. That they will be any more successful in the future is practically unthinkable. Stronger, both relatively and actually, than before the War, the British Navy calmly awaits "the day," hoping it may soon come, when the Germans will stake their existence upon a last desperate effort to challenge that mastery of the sea the hope of which must be slipping for ever from their grasp.

It is only necessary to say a few words about the atrocious policy of submarine "frightfulness" which culminated in the sinking of the "Lusitania" and the deliberate sacrifice of the lives of some 1,200 innocent people who had nothing whatever to do with the War. That policy, the deluded German people were solemnly assured, was to bring Britain to her knees by cutting off supplies of food and raw material, and starving her into submission. It is worth noting in this connection that the Germans to-day are calling upon heaven and earth to punish the brutal English for attempting to "starve the German people" by a perfectly legitimate blockade carried out in strict accordance with the rules of international law. We heard nothing of the iniquities of the "starvation" policy as long as the Germans hoped to be able to apply it to us in the same way that they applied it to Paris during the war of 1870-71; it was only when they realised that the submarine policy had failed that they began the desperate series of appeals, directed especially to the United States, that they were being unfairly treated owing to Britain refusing to allow them the "freedom of the seas"—in other words, refusing to sit idly by while Germany obtained from the United States and elsewhere the food and munitions of which she stood, and stands, in such desperate need.

As a matter of fact, the German submarine campaign has not even succeeded in reducing appreciably the strength of the British mercantile marine.

Despite our losses, our mercantile marine is to-day, thanks to new building and purchases, but little weaker than when war broke out, while, so far as we can judge, the submarine campaign has failed to contribute in the slightest degree to the rise in food values which has imposed so great a burden upon large classes of people in our country. It has been in fact, a complete and absolute failure. It has cost us, it is true, many valuable vessels and many valuable lives, but as a means to ending the War it has achieved practically nothing. The policy of terrifying by murder has prospered no more afloat than it did ashore, while outside the ranks of the combatants it has done nothing but earn for Germany the contempt of the whole civilised world, to bring Germany within an ace of war with the United States, and to brand the German Navy and the entire German nation with an indelible stain of blood and crime.

The submarine policy was a policy which could have been justified only by complete success. It may suit the German Press, led by the nose by the Government, to tell the German people that hated England was being rapidly subdued by the efforts of the "heroic" murderers commanding the German U-boats. We know differently.

We have the authority of Mr Balfour for saying that the German losses in submarines have been "formidable," and it has been stated—and not contradicted—in the House of Commons that no fewer than fifty of these assassins of the sea have met the fate which their infamy richly deserved. Unofficial estimates have put the number even higher. We shall not know the exact facts until after the War, but we know at least that the German people have at length awakened to an uneasy realisation of the fact that they have murdered in vain, and that they have covered themselves with undying infamy to no real purpose.

I do not suppose that knowledge sits very hardly upon their consciences; but even in Germany there must be people who are beginning to wonder what judgment the civilised world will pass upon them in the future, and how they are ever to hold up their heads again among civilised nations. And not even a German can remain perpetually indifferent to the judgment of the civilised world.

By every means which ingenuity could devise and daring seamanship could carry into execution Germany's submarines have been chased, harried, and sunk, until, as we are informed upon reliable authority, the chiefs of the German Navy are finding it increasingly difficult to find and train submarine crews. And small wonder! No one questions the bravery of the German sailor, whatever we may think of his humanity. But, also, he is human, and not the superhuman being which the Germans imagine themselves to be. And when he sees, week after week and month after month, submarine after submarine venturing forth into the waters of the North Sea only to be mysteriously swallowed up in the void, one can understand that he shrinks appalled from a prospect sufficient to shake the nerves of men who, whatever their other qualities may be, have not been bred for hundreds of years to the traditions and the dangers of the sea. Small wonder that they quail from the unknown fate which for ever threatens them! Many sally forth never to return; others, more fortunate, on reaching home have a tale to tell which, losing nothing in the telling, is not of a nature to encourage their fellows.

It is said that a single voyage in a German submarine is enough so seriously to try the nerves of officers and men that they need a prolonged rest before they are ready to resume their duties. Imagine the conditions under which they live! Hunted day and night by the relentless British destroyers, faced ever by strange and unfamiliar perils and by traps of which they know nothing, it is hardly a matter of surprise if their nerves give way.

The War has given us the most wonderful example the world has ever seen of what sea power means. Thanks to their undisputed command of the ocean, the Allies have been able to carry on operations in widely separated theatres practically free from any of the difficulties which would certainly have proved insurmountable in the presence of strong hostile forces afloat. We and our Allies have been able to transport men and munitions wherever we wished without serious hindrance, and even in the presence of hostile submarines we have only lost two or three transports in eighteen months of war. That, it must be admitted, is a very wonderful record.

Even the tragic blunder of the Dardanelles gave us a striking instance of what sea power can effect. We were able, thanks to the Navy, not merely to land huge forces in the face of the enemy, but we were able also to re-embark them without loss under circumstances which, by all the laws of war, should have meant an appalling list of casualties. There can be no doubt whatever that had the re-embarking troops on the Gallipoli Pensinsula tried to reach their ships without having firm command of the sea, not more than a very small percentage of them would have survived.

In considering the bearings of naval power to the great struggle as a whole, we must always keep in mind what the Germans expected and hoped when they declared war. We know, of course, that they did not expect Britain to enter the War. But at the same time they must have realised that there was a possibility of our doing so, and they had formulated a plan of campaign to meet such a contingency. We know pretty well what that campaign was. The German theory has been put into practice since; unfortunately for the Germans, it has not worked out quite in accordance with the text-books. They declared for the "war of attrition"; their idea was that, by submarine attacks, the British Fleet could be so whittled down that at length the German main Fleet would be able to meet it with reasonable prospects of success. Their Fleet, while the process of attrition was going on, was to remain sheltered in the unreachable fastnesses of the Kiel Canal. The latter, however, is the only part of the German programme which has gone according to the book.

The "High Canal Fleet" remains in the "last ditch," and apparently, at the time of writing, seems likely to remain there. But the process of attrition has not made the progress the Germans hoped for. It is true we have lost a number of ships through submarine attacks. But it will not be overlooked by the Germans any more than by ourselves that the greater part of our losses was sustained in the early days of the submarine campaign. As soon as the Navy "got busy" with the submarine pest our losses practically ceased, and it is now a long time since we have lost a fighting unit through torpedo attack. As is usual with the Navy, our men set themselves to grapple with unfamiliar conditions, and their success has been very striking. Not only have they been able to protect themselves against submarine attack, but they have made the home seas, at any rate, too hot to hold the pirates, dozens of which have been destroyed or captured. And when the submarine war was transferred to the Mediterranean it was not very long before the Navy again had the menace well in hand. In the meantime our building programme was pushed forward at such a rate that a very large number of ships of the most powerful class have been added to the fighting units of the Fleet, with the result that not merely relatively to the Fleet of Germany, but actually in point of ships, men, and guns, our Fleet to-day is stronger than it was when war broke out. That, again, is an achievement wholly without parallel. And it is one of the chief factors in considering the future of the campaign. The Germans have never been able to rival us in speed of construction even in times of peace; it is in the last degree unlikely that they have been able to do so under the conditions that have prevailed during the past eighteen months. I have not the least doubt that we are fully justified in assuming that our final victory at sea is assured—if, indeed, it is not practically won already. The conditions are plain for everyone, both at home and abroad, to see for himself, and we have plenty of evidence to suggest that they are fully appreciated in Germany; the idle quays of Hamburg, the idle fleets of German merchant ships rotting in the shelter of neutral ports, the peaceful progress of the ships of the Allies over the seas of the world, and the growing stringency of conditions in Germany brought about by the British blockade are quite sufficient evidence for those Germans—and their number is growing—who are no longer blinded by the national megalomania.

Our Navy is a silent service; it would perhaps be better for us if at times it were a little more vocal. For there is no disguising the fact that there is a body of impatient grumblers at home who, because we do not read of a great sea victory every morning with our breakfasts, are apt to ask what the Navy is doing. We can be quite sure that that question is not asked in Germany. There, at any rate, the answer is plain.

We can discount, I am sure, the tales we hear of Germany starving, and that the horrors of Paris in 1870 are being repeated. That story is no doubt diligently spread abroad by the Germans themselves in the hope of appealing to the sentiment, or rather the sentimentality, of certain classes in the neutral nations. At the same time, we cannot shut our eyes to the growing mass of evidence which goes to show that the stringency of the British blockade is producing a great and increasing effect throughout Germany. To begin with, her export trade, despite the leaks in the blockade, has practically vanished, and it must be remembered that modern Germany is the creation of trade with overseas countries. She grew rich on commerce; she might have grown richer if she had been content with the opportunities which were as fully open to her as to the rest of the world. It is due to the steady strangling process carried out by the British Navy that her long accumulation of wealth has been decisively checked, and that she is dissipating that accumulation in what is inevitably bound to be a sure, if slow, bleeding to death. And, whatever may be the course of the War, Germany's overseas trade can be resumed only by the permission or through the destruction of the British Navy. That is a factor of supreme and tremendous importance.

In the British blockade—in other words, in the British Fleet—we have the factor which in the long run must make possible the final overthrow of Germany. I am not suggesting that we can win this war by sea power alone; the final crash must come through the defeat of Germany's land forces, since she is a land and not a sea Power. But it is the operation of sea power which must make the final blow possible. Sea power, and sea power alone, will make possible the final blockade of Germany by land as well as by sea. The ring of the blockade already is nearly complete; and when the British and French, advancing from the base at Salonica, link up, as they must sooner or later, with the Russian forces coming south across the Balkans, Germany will be held in a ring of iron from which she will have no means of escape.

She realises fully that she has not the remotest chance of breaking through the lines of the Allies in the West; she has failed utterly to break the Russian line in the East. It is vital for her to break the ring by which she is nearly surrounded, and in this fact we have the explanation of her dash across the Balkans. So far that dash has been attended with a great measure of success owing to the failure of the Allies to win the active support of Greece, Rumania, and Bulgaria. She has succeeded in crushing Serbia and Montenegro, and in linking up with her Turkish Allies through the medium of the Constantinople railway. But Salonica, firmly held by the Allies, must ever be a thorn in the side of her progress to the East, and until she succeeds in reducing it her flank is open to a blow which would shatter her prospects in the East as decisively as they have already been shattered in the West. We cannot imagine that the Allies have gone to Salonica solely for reasons of their health, and it needs no great acquaintance with military history to realise that the possession by the Allies of the Salonica lines may be as fatal to Germany as the holding of the lines of Torres Vedras by Wellington was fatal to the plans of Napoleon.

The analogy is not exact—analogies seldom are—but "the Spanish ulcer" is sufficiently reproduced for practical purposes. German commanders in the East can never feel safe so long as Salonica remains in our possession. And I have no doubt that when the time is ripe we shall see the Allies advancing through the Balkans to join hands with the Russians and, it may be, with the Rumanians. Then Germany will be definitely isolated, and the process of exhaustion, already considerably advanced, will proceed with ever-growing momentum, until it reaches the point when a combined attack on land by the whole of the Allies simultaneously will prove irresistible. I am not one of those who believe that Germany can be defeated by economic pressure alone. But it cannot be denied that economic pressure offers the greatest means of so weakening her power of resistance that her final military defeat will be rendered immeasurably easier.

And we must always remember—there is too strong a tendency in certain quarters to forget it—that it is the principal duty of the British Navy, so long as the German Fleet prefers idleness to fighting, to bring about the reduction of the German power of resistance by a remorseless strangulation of her trade. Our policy in this respect is perfectly definite. It is that, paying due regard to the undoubted rights of neutral nations, we will allow nothing to reach Germany which will assist to prolong her powers of resistance.

There has been a strong disposition in some quarters to represent the British Navy as fighting with one hand tied behind its back owing to the supposed apathy or worse of the Foreign Office. Sir Edward Grey, in perhaps the greatest speech of his long career, has sufficiently disposed of that charge. It is not denied that from a variety of causes, some of them at least beyond our control, Germany has obtained supplies which we would very gladly have denied to her. But, unfortunately for us and fortunately for her, neutral nations have their rights, which we are bound to respect unless we wish to make fresh enemies. It is beyond doubt that supplies are leaking into Germany through Holland and Scandinavia which we should be glad to keep out. It is absolutely impossible to prove enemy destination in all these cases, and it must be remembered that unless we can prove this we have no right to interfere with the commerce of neutral nations, who are quite entitled, if they can do so, to supply Germany with precisely the class of goods which the United States is supplying to us.

We are too apt to overlook the fact that there is nothing criminal in supplying guns and ammunition to Germany. Neutral nations are free to do so—if they can. We are entitled to stop them—also if we can. But we are not entitled to interfere with the legitimate commerce of a neutral nation; in other words, we must prove that contraband is intended for the use of the enemy before we can lay hands upon it.

It is this feature of international law which makes it so difficult for us to declare an absolute blockade of Germany. And it is just this aspect of the case which is the justification of the trade agreements of the kind which has been concluded with Denmark. Under that agreement, and under similar ones, we allow certain goods to be imported in normal volume to neutral countries under the assurance that they will not be re-exported to Germany. The agreement with Denmark has been violently attacked, and attacked, as everyone admits who has seen it, without the slightest justification. It is admitted that it does not give us all we would like to have; but, on the other hand, it is also admitted by those who have seen it that it gives us a good deal more than we could hope to obtain by other means short of what would be practically a declaration of war.

And even the hotheads among us would shrink from telling either Holland or the Scandinavian countries that unless they surrender their rights and do as we wish, we should at once declare war upon them or practically force them to declare war upon us. We need have no shadow of doubt what Germany would do if she wielded the power we do. She would show, as she has shown, scant consideration for the rights of neutrals. But, thank heaven! we are not Germany, and we fight with clean hands.

We have to solve the problem of making our blockade as effectual as possible while paying scrupulous regard to the rights of others. That problem is in process of solution; the importation of commodities into Germany is decreasing day by day; and if we are not at the end of our difficulties in this respect, we are at least drawing into sight of the achievement of our purpose. And the more fully that purpose can be attained, the nearer draws the end of the great struggle and the emancipation of the civilised world from the dominion of brute force.

Chapter Three
The Coming Victory on Land

No one in these days would seek to minimise the untold advantages which sea power confers upon those who wield it.

But to say that England, supreme at sea, could conquer Germany while the latter was undefeated on land would be to stretch the doctrine of sea power very far beyond what is actually within the bounds of possibility. Very few people to-day hold the doctrines of sea power which were current coin only a few months ago. That without sea power Germany could win a decisive victory over England is admittedly impossible.

Without sea power greater than our own she can neither destroy our trade nor attempt an invasion of England with any prospect of success. In the presence of the British Fleet any attempt to land on these shores sufficient forces to act with decisive effect would be impossible. For such an undertaking Germany must secure command of the narrow seas, even though it might be for only a few days or even a few hours.

Under existing conditions her sole chance of doing this would be to decoy our Fleet away from our home waters by a desperate dash of her own squadrons, trusting to be able to carry out a surprise landing on our shores in the interval—necessarily brief—in which she could hope to operate undisturbed. That menace, however, is one to which the chiefs of our Navy are fully awake, and it is indeed a forlorn hope.

Imagine Germany successful on land. Could we defeat her through our undisputed command of the sea? Personally I do not believe we could. In all probability she could under such circumstances obtain the supplies which would render her self-supporting, while at the same time doing a great trade with neutral nations or with her former antagonists over the land routes which we could not command.

It is for this reason that the situation calls for the exercise of military power on the part of Britain on a scale never dreamed of in previous years.

We may, I think, take it for granted that without the military as well as the naval assistance of Great Britain our Allies would have very little prospect of bringing the War to a successful conclusion. It is the military power of England, growing gradually day by day, which in the end must turn the scale if the scale is to be turned. It is true we have rendered to our Allies very much more than the measure of support which we promised them when we joined them to combat the peril which threatened all in common. We have rendered the seas safe; we have already given assistance on land perhaps far beyond anything they either expected or had the right to ask. Naturally, we make no special virtue of this; the fight is one of self-preservation for ourselves just as it is for France, Russia, and Italy. We all share a common peril; all of us in common owe to the others the fullest mutual co-operation and effort.

And upon us, just as much as upon our Allies, rests the duty of developing our fighting efficiency to the highest pitch of which the Empire is capable. Nothing less than this will be sufficient to remove for all time the menace by which civilisation is faced. Those who say that because Britain has gone beyond what she undertook to do it cannot be expected that she should do more are nothing less than traitors to the common cause. We cannot bargain with our destiny. And, assuredly, if we fail to measure the gravity of the situation, if we fail to put forth the whole energies of our people, destiny will take a terrible revenge. Can it be, with the awful lessons of Belgium and Serbia before our eyes, that this nation will be satisfied with anything less than the maximum of effort in the prosecution of the War?

Cost what it may, the final overthrow of Germany must be effected *on land*, and in the execution of that inflexible purpose Britain, whether she likes it or not, must play a leading part. We have been for centuries a great naval Power; the day has dawned when we must become a great military Power as well. We have, indeed, already become so in part. We have raised armies on a scale which, before the War, neither our friends nor our enemies would have thought possible. Without unduly flattering ourselves, we may claim to have done much; we shall yet do more and more until the power of Prussia is finally broken. It is not enough that we should content ourselves, as some suggest, with supplying money and munitions to our Allies.

We must take the field as a nation fighting for everything which makes life worth living. To those who say that we cannot afford to raise larger armies than we have already raised, I would reply that if necessary the last of Britain's savings, the whole strength of her manhood, must be flung into the melting-pot of war. And I am happy to think that at length the nation as a whole is showing a growing realisation of this undoubted fact. We are fast getting over our preliminary troubles (which have lasted far too long); the entire nation is settling down in grim and deadly earnest to make an end once and for all of the German pretensions. "Tear-'em is a good dog, but Holdfast is better," says the old saw, and we are to-day not far from the time when, not for the first time in the world's history, the silent, deadly, dogged determination of the British race will be a fact with which the entire world will have to reckon. We are out to fight this War to a finish, and I am glad to think the nation as a whole has at last awakened to the grim facts of the situation.

Those who are suggesting that the British Navy can by any means give the death-blow to German aim at world-domination are, I am convinced, doing the nation ill service. Their argument is that because we are a naval Power we should be content with the exercise of our naval strength, and should not venture to embark on military operations on a scale for which our previous experience has not tended to fit us. Counsels of this kind, however well intended, are a profound—they might well be a fatal—mistake. They tend to deaden the brain and paralyse the arm of the Executive; they add to the terrible perils by which we are already surrounded. More than this, they tend greatly to prolong the conflict and add immeasurably to the terrible toll of life and treasure which the War is extorting from all the nations who have the misfortune to be engaged in it. Let us put aside once and for all the comfortable theory that as we have already done more than was expected of us there is no need for further exertions.

There is a crying need for all that we can do, for more, indeed, than we can hope to do.

To be sparing of effort in war is to be guilty of the greatest possible folly. Moderation in war, as Lord Fisher is credited with saying, is imbecility; and it is infinitely cheaper in the long run to do a thing well than to half do it and, probably, have all the work to do over again under still more difficult circumstances, even if it can be done at all. A glance at the record of the Dardanelles Expedition will show what I mean.

And unless in this hour of supreme trial Britain is true to herself and to the great cause for which she and her Allies have unsheathed the sword, if she is content with less than the utmost effort of which she is capable, the historian of the future, looking backward across the centuries, will be able to place his finger unerringly upon the day and hour of which it will be possible to say, "Here the decline of the British Empire began." Happily, indeed, for ourselves and civilisation at large the awakening spirit of our people is the best possible guarantee against any such disaster.

As I said in my opening chapter, our mythical visitor from another planet, judging the progress of the War by the map only, might well be excused if he came to the conclusion that the Germans had already won so far as the land campaign was concerned. Now this is precisely the mental position of the German people to-day. They have been told, day by day and month by month, that Germany is everywhere victorious, and, speaking generally, they believe it. Of course, a few of the more thoughtful and better informed are beginning to wonder why, if the constant tales of victory are true, they seem to be no nearer to the sight of peace. But the German Government has to deal not with the well-informed few, but with the ill-informed many.

So long as the mass of the people are prepared to believe what they are told, they will go on supplying the Government with the means of war, and, after all, that is no bad frame of mind for the conduct of a great struggle.

No doubt the process of disillusionment, when it comes, will be all the more violent and painful, but at present we have to face the fact that a very large proportion of the German people believe that they are winning. Up to recently they have shown that they are willing to put up with the shortage and distress which are growing in Germany, looking upon them as part of the price of victory. But, as I shall show later, even this comfortable belief is beginning to break down before the stern logic of facts, and, as a result, chinks and cracks are appearing even in the iron wall of German patience and perseverance. That those chinks and cracks will widen as time goes on is certain; and when the wall gives way, as it assuredly will, we shall see a catastrophe which will probably sweep away the German organisation as it exists to-day.

Now let us consider for a moment the grounds upon which Germany assumes she has won the War. She regards the whole field of the War on land as absolutely dominated by the German arms. German armies have occupied practically the whole of Belgium, they have pushed their way far into France, they have occupied the whole of Poland and a considerable slice of Russia proper, they have overrun and devastated Serbia and Montenegro, have won control of the Balkans, and have opened up an uninterrupted way to Constantinople and the East. But—and it is a very big "but" indeed—their one complete military success in the real sense of the word has been the destruction of the fighting power of Montenegro, the smallest and the weakest of their opponents! Not even Serbia, properly speaking, has been destroyed as a fighting force, for at least half of the splendid Serbian Army is intact, and will take the field again as soon as it has rested and secured fresh equipment.

As regards Germany's more powerful opponents, the only ones which count so far as the final decision of the War is concerned, they stand to-day not merely with their fighting efficiency unimpaired, but, taken as a whole, actually stronger than they were a year ago. The huge armies which

Britain is raising have not yet even taken the field; France is certainly no more weakened relatively than is Germany herself; Russia, recovering amazingly from her misfortunes, will soon be ready to strike new and harder blows; Italy is steadily, if slowly, pushing forward to the heart of her hereditary enemy. Moreover, all are absolutely united and determined in the prosecution of the War.

Yet in the face of these indisputable facts the Germans appear to be genuinely surprised that the Allies are not ready and willing to accept the preposterous "peace terms" which, in their arrogance, they have been good enough to put forward, through the usual "unofficial" channels, for acceptance. It is a surprise to them that the Allies are not ready to confess that they are vanquished. The fact is, of course, that they are not vanquished or anything like it. They mean to go on, as Mr Asquith has said, until the military power of Prussia, the *fons et origo* of the whole bloody struggle, is finally and completely destroyed. And they have the means and the will to do it. The fact that Germany has forced her way into so large an amount of the Allied territory is merely, in the eyes of the Allies, another reason why they should continue to fight, and a good reason why they should fight with growing hopes of ultimate success.

Longer lines necessarily mean thinner lines, for the simple reason that Germany has reused her maximum of man-power, while the Allies have still large reserves as yet untouched.

There we have the bedrock fact of the War, and no amount of boasting and bragging of German "victories" will alter it. It signifies little or nothing that Germany shall have overrun the Balkans so long as she is open to a smashing blow in the West, which is, and must ever be to the end, the real heart of the War. It is in France and Flanders that the final blow must come, and it will profit Germany nothing to hold Constantinople while the Allies are thundering at the crossing of the Rhine.

If Germany had succeeded in her ambitious design to capture Paris or London or Petrograd, she might have reasonable excuse for some of the boasting which has filled the columns of her Press; she would have still more excuse if she had succeeded in destroying the armed forces of Britain or of France or of Russia. But she has done none of these things. Britain, France, Russia, and Italy are not merely still full of fight, they are growing stronger while she is growing weaker. They are certainly not weakening as much as she is herself in the moral sense and in the capacity and determination to endure to the end. And while I am no believer in the theory that a war can be won by sitting down and waiting for exhaustion to defeat the enemy, there can be no doubt of the fact that if the War resolves itself into a contest of endurance the Allies are at least as well equipped as the Germans to see this thing through to the end.

We must never lose sight of the fact that the German thrust to the East is merely an expression of her uncomfortable consciousness that it is her last chance of breaking the blockade by land as well as by sea which is exercising such a strangling effect upon her. Germany, as a fact, is in the position of a beleaguered garrison. Unless she can break the ring around her she must inevitably perish. If we bear this fact in mind, we shall be in a better position to appreciate at its real value the bearing of the German successes in the direction of Constantinople, and of her real motives in that adventure. So far Germany is closely blockaded on three fronts—by the French and British, by the Italians, and by the Russians. She can have no reasonable hope that she will be able to break the blockade in either of these directions; her efforts have already brought her disastrous failures and enormous losses. By her success in the Balkans she has opened, for what they are worth, fresh sources of supplies; she has secured, again for what it is worth, the adhesion of Bulgaria; she has secured the neutrality of Greece, and, so far, of Rumania. But she is not yet safe even here. Salonica menaces her communications eastwards; and should the Allies take the offensive from this base, we ought to see the last of Germany's communications with the outer world, except through the neutral countries, finally closed. Then, and then only, will the full influence of the sea power of the Allies begin to make itself felt with decisive results.

The plain fact is that those who have decried the supposed inactivity of the British Fleet have failed to take into consideration the fact that the German successes on land have, to some extent, neutralised British successes afloat. Germany had every reason to hope that our failure in the Gallipoli Peninsula would enable her to call upon the services of some half a million Turks and to secure fresh sources of supplies of food and raw material, not very great, perhaps, but still helpful; and in Serbia she has won what is of real value, a fresh supply of copper. If she could push through a really serviceable system of communication with Bagdad and the Persian Gulf, she would gain still more solid advantages, including, it might be, control of the British oil supplies in Persia. But this hope has been utterly smashed by the great Russian victory at Erzerum. I do not believe the German aims in these directions were immediate perils, but the Germans, as we know to our cost, take long views in matters of war, and the better we understand their aims the better will be our chance of countering them. And in this case a full understanding of what Germany is aiming at provides us with a specially urgent reason for decisive action at the point where Germany can be hit the hardest. This is unquestionably on the West front.

The importance of closing at the earliest possible moment the gap in the blockade—the direct road from Berlin to Constantinople and Egypt and the East—is supreme, for Germany may very veil secure, if only for a time, complete control of Turkey. The effect of our sea power is gravely weakened if Germany is able to draw the supplies of men and materials she needs through the Balkan countries. We have to re-establish the barrier on the Eastern road with as little delay as possible, remembering that the Germans may be trusted to make the utmost of what must seem to our foes to be nothing less than a heaven-sent opportunity. We know that already they have very completely looted Serbia of everything that could be of the slightest use to them, and we can be fairly confident that the process will be continued in Turkey and Bulgaria.

It is for this reason that the Balkan area suddenly assumed such importance in the War. So long as Germany keeps open the road to the East, so long is she obtaining reinforcements in men and supplies which enable her to prolong the War.

There are a variety of plans open to us for the purpose of countering the latest German thrust for the open. But it must be remembered that the majority of these partake too much of the nature of the "small packet" to be sound from a military and strategic point of view. Most of our troubles in the present War have sprung from a diffusion of effort which has led us to dissipate our strength in a variety of local attacks which have missed the point at which a decisive blow could be dealt.

We have over and over again been too weak at the critical point. That is a danger which I trust will be guarded against in the future by the improved arrangements that have been made during the past few months for a better co-ordination of the joint plans of the Allies. Joint simultaneous action by all the Allies, each on his own front, is one of the cardinal necessities for bringing the War to a successful conclusion, and unless this is attained we shall always be faced with the danger that Germany, having the advantage of operating on interior lines, will be able, thanks to the mobility afforded her by her magnificent system of railways, to meet and check, if not to defeat, her enemies in detail.

It is an unhappy fact that so far there has been a lamentable lack of co-ordination between the Allies. For some reason or another we have never been able to bring our preparations to fruition at the same moment. Valuable steps have been taken of late, however, to bring about a better co-ordination of the Allies' plans, and there is therefore reason to hope that in the coming great struggle we shall see greater unity of action as well as more unity of control and direction.

But whatever may be the success of our efforts in this direction I have not the least doubt that the West front will remain the decisive theatre of the War. If the Germans are to be beaten, they will be beaten in the West; if we can score a great success there, we can with every confidence leave the Balkan imbroglio and the menace to Egypt and the East to settle itself. A strong threat in the direction of the Rhine would bring the German armies westward as fast as express trains could carry them, would automatically open up the road across the Balkans from Salonica, and would at once enormously facilitate the Russian recovery of lost territory and an invasion of Germany from the East.

Moreover, it would be a blow in the decisive direction, for, after all—and it cannot be too often repeated—it is on the Western front that the final victory will be won.

Now there can be no doubt that the Germans themselves are fully conscious of this fact, and that they are taking the speediest measures to guard against the peril of a great attack by the Allies in the course of the coming months. The Budapest correspondent of the *Morning Post* has given us invaluable information upon this point. Great developments are expected in Austro-German military circles in the early spring, and preparations are being made to meet a tremendous onslaught by the Allies on three or four fronts. One of the best informed military writers in Hungary, Monsieur Tibor Bakos, who is known to have exceptional sources of information, has stated that in the early spring the Allied Powers have decided to embark upon an offensive of unparalleled magnitude. This is the direct result of the steps that have been taken to establish a common military and diplomatic leadership and control among the Allies. They know well in Vienna and Berlin that at a given moment the iron ring round the Central Empires will suddenly tighten at every point.

"All the political leaders and generals of the Allies," says the writer, "are absolutely certain of a great and decisive victory, and their optimism as regards the final issue of the War is even more marked than it was in 1914, when the War began, and in the spring of 1915, when Italy joined the Entente."

Now, assuming that a joint scheme of attack has been decided upon, where will these attacks be delivered? That, of course, is the secret of our military leaders; but, within certain lines, there is ground for a reasonable forecast. And first and foremost comes the battle-ground in the West. In this direction Champagne and Artois seem clearly marked out. The Russians may be expected to move on both wings of their long lines—in the south with the idea of joining hands with the French and British across the

Balkans and of convincing Rumania, and in the north to complete a turning movement which shall drive back the German centre. On the Italian front the line of the Isonzo seems to be indicated.

As supplementary but still important movements we shall probably see shrewd blows struck across Macedonia and at Turkey in the Caucasus, and perhaps elsewhere. Indeed, the blow at Erzerum has come since these lines were penned.

On the other hand, we have to remember that the Germans may anticipate our blows at any or all of these points. What are the prospects of success for us or for our enemies?

Now we are assured by those who ought to know that the strength of the Allies in men and munitions is greater than that of the enemy. We are assured that our supplies of shells are now fully adequate, and it is a remarkable fact that a writer in a leading American magazine has stated recently that we are no longer ordering shells from the United States. We know that we and the French have vast supplies of guns. Can we, with all these advantages, break decisively the German lines in the West, which the enemy professes to regard as impregnable?

I believe we can, and I believe it is in the West that the real and most deadly blow will come. No doubt it will be coupled with strong action elsewhere, but I have seen and heard nothing to shake my conviction that here must be the real settlement of the War. Given ample supplies of men and guns and ammunition, I believe we have commanders who are capable of driving the enemy out of his strong entrenchments from the North Sea to the Swiss frontier, who are capable of forcing the crossing of the Rhine and carrying the War into the enemy's territory. And we must always remember that Germany is peculiarly sensitive to invasion. We know something of the panic that was caused by the Russian advance into East Prussia in the early days of the War. And since then the Germans have begun to fear that in the event of invasion the measure that they have meted out to those they had in their power will in turn be meted out to themselves. They have, in fact, a bad conscience, and they fear the vengeance of their foes.

In this, as in all other wars, one is faced with the fact that the written word of to-day may be falsified by the events of to-morrow, but as I write there is every indication that we are on the eve of a renewal of the great struggle which shall go far to decide on the Western front the issue of the War. Already we hear the mutterings which prelude the breaking of the storm. We hear of German guns and reinforcements hurrying westward, we know that our own commanders are not idle, we know that the "deadlock" is more apparent than real, and that in war, as in everything else, nothing ever really stands still. Every day that passes helps us or our enemies. We cannot say that the coming struggle will give us all we seek; we know that in any event we have many days of trial and grievous loss before us. But we have good grounds for hope. Our people are united and determined to an extent to which we have hitherto been strangers.

We know that everything has been done to fit our troops to play their great part in what may well be the final act of Armageddon. We know they are resolute and of good courage. And if the coming great battle of the West, of which to-day we hear and see the signs, prove, as it well may, the most terrible conflict which this old earth has ever witnessed, we can look forward with calm confidence to the outcome, for we believe that Britain and France, united and determined, confident in the justice of their cause, will be far more than a match for any effort our enemies can make either in offence or defence. If we can secure united and simultaneous action by all the Allies, it is my firm belief that before the year is out we shall have set our advancing feet on the road which leads to Berlin and victory.

Chapter Four
Our Mastery of the Air

The story of the British air service in the days before the War is so characteristically English that I must give a few lines to it if only to make quite clear the realisation of what we have done to meet the new dangers which, as usual, caught us unprepared.

We exhibited as a nation a most regrettable reluctance to comprehend the value of the aeroplane and the airship as a means of making war.

We failed utterly to grasp the fact that with the coming of the aeroplane a new factor had entered into military science, just as, in the early days of the submarine, we neglected the new invention until we had lagged behind other nations to an extent that, under different circumstances, might well have proved disastrous. We made a few feeble and futile efforts in aeroplane construction; we dallied tentatively with airships of a microscopic pattern. The flying wing of the Army was half starved, and the advice and remonstrances of the men who had really studied and understood the subject were cold-shouldered by the authorities to whom everything new and revolutionary was—and too often is—anathema.

I have studied the progress of aviation from the time when I acted as a judge at the first Aviation Meeting held in this country—on Doncaster racecourse. It may perhaps be remembered that in the early days of flying, when the *Daily Mail* offered a prize of 10,000 pounds for the first flight from London to Manchester, a misguided evening journal derisively offered a prize of a million pounds for the first man who flew, I think, ten miles.

No doubt the sneer was inspired partly by professional jealousy of the *Daily Mail*, but it revealed, in very striking fashion, the mental attitude, shared unfortunately by our military authorities, of those who refused to see in the new arm anything more than a very complicated, useless, and dangerous toy.

Time has slipped along since Sommer, Le Blon, and Cody flew at Doncaster; the pioneers of aviation persisted in their efforts, and within three years of the *Daily Mail's* offer being made the prize had been won. Tremendous progress was made in every department of flying, and the keener students of military affairs realised that in the aeroplane there had arrived a weapon, both of offence and defence, which would go far to revolutionise warfare as it had been understood in the past.

None the less, our Army lagged far behind the rest of the world. Either the War authorities were not sufficiently insistent, or the Treasury turned a deaf ear to their appeals for money for the development of the new science.

The result was that while our French friends and our German enemies—for they were our enemies even then, as we have now good reason to know—were pushing ahead with aerial investigation and securing a lead which might well have been fatal to us, the British air service languished in comparative neglect. It is certainly hardly too much to say that but for the assistance given by the *Daily Mail* flying in England would have been utterly and totally neglected. The result was what might have been expected, and the outcome was characteristically British.

When the War broke out we were in a condition of decided inferiority to the French fliers—that perhaps mattered little, as we were fighting on the same side—and very much behindhand in relation to Germany, which mattered a great deal. We had to make up in quality—and of the quality of our airmen there was happily no question—what we lacked in equipment. We were entirely without airships comparable in any way to the Zeppelins, and we had nothing like the number of the German "Tauben." Most happily for us the quality of our airmen proved far beyond anything which Germany possesses, and in the matter of men we took at once, and have since held, a commanding lead.

It was not long before the value of the new arm was signally demonstrated. In all probability the fate of the British Army in the early days of the War was decided by air reconnaissance. It was one of the air scouts who discovered the enormous concentration of German troops before Sir John French's army, and thus gave the timely warning which made the great retreat from Mons a possibility.

What followed reproduced in striking fashion the early history of the submarine, and proved very clearly that our deficiencies in the matter of aircraft were not due to any defect in personnel or energy or inventiveness. Striking advances were made when the obvious requirements of the War became manifest.

Money, of course, had to be poured out like water, and no doubt we spent a great deal more than would have been necessary had we made due preparation in time of peace. But, at any rate, thanks to the British genius for improvisation, the work was done. Men and machines were soon forthcoming in ever-increasing numbers, and it was not many months before Sir John French was able to announce that our airmen had established a definite personal ascendency over the airmen of the enemy. That ascendency has been fully maintained.

Man for man and machine for machine we lead the Germans in the matter of flight, so far at least as the aeroplane is concerned. German losses in aerial conflict have been very much heavier than our own, a fact that is not surprising when the personal equation is taken into consideration. In natural daring and personal initiative—two of the qualities indispensable to the successful airman—the French and the British characters are far superior to the German. We can look forward with complete confidence to any comparison that can be made between the rival air services so far as the heavier-than-air machines are concerned.

A good deal has been said lately about the new German Fokker machine, and there has been a good deal of loose talk as to its formidable possibilities. As a matter of fact, its wonders appear to have been very much exaggerated, for it is only a powerful engine put into an obsolete type of French machine. It is not without significance that it is designed for purely defensive purposes, and is absolutely forbidden to cross the German lines under any circumstances whatever. It is a very small, very heavily engined monoplane, carrying a formidable gun, and for short distances capable of very swift climbing and very high speed.

For its own special purpose it is undoubtedly a first-class engine of war, but that it has met its match in the British and French battle-planes was clearly shown during a recent raid on Freiburg. During that raid, a great part of which was over enemy territory, the fighting machines which acted as escorts to the bombers fought no fewer than ten battles with the Fokkers and Aviatiks; and when we remember that the only aeroplane of the Allies to be lost out of the entire squadron was compelled to descend through engine trouble, we can easily understand that highly exaggerated reports as to the efficiency of the rule-of-thumb Fokker had by some means got into circulation. In all probability they arose from the comparatively numerous victims among our flying men claimed by the German official news just after the Fokker made its appearance. But the reason for the seeming disproportion in numbers was very simple. We were constantly the attacking party; in other words, our airmen were constantly over the German lines, while the Germans, as far as they could, gave our lines a very wide berth. The following figures, quoted in the House of Commons by Mr Tennant, are illuminating. They relate to four weeks' fighting on the Western front, practically all of which had taken place in German territory:

British machines lost, 13.
Enemy machines brought down, 9.
Enemy machines probably brought down, 2.
British bombing raids, 6.
Enemy bombing raids, 13.
British machines used, 138.
Enemy machines used, about 20.
Machines flown across enemy lines, 1227.
Enemy machines flown across our lines (estimated), 310.

Now we need not go farther than these figures to see that the apparently heavier British losses are due not to any superiority on the German side, but to the enormously greater risks taken by our men. They are constantly flying over the German lines, whereas the German airman appears—probably with good reason—to keep to the comparative safety of his own territory, where he is protected by the German anti-aircraft guns. And that when it comes to actual combat in the air the British battle-plane has little to fear from the Fokker is shown by the experience of one of our airmen who single-handed fought a duel with three Fokkers and brought them all down. Moreover, we have always to remember that when a battle is fought the defeated Fokker comes to earth in German territory, and we cannot definitely count it as destroyed, whereas if one of our machines is brought down the Germans are always as sure of it as we are.

Another factor which shows how great an advantage we have over the enemy in the matter of the air service is revealed by the comparative failure of German bombing attacks and the havoc that has been wrought by the French and British squadrons. Leaving the Zeppelin raids for the moment out of the question, there can be no difference of opinion that the Allies' air raids have been enormously the more destructive, not in the matter of the sacrifice of civilian life—pre-eminence in that regard is easily claimed by the Huns—but in the havoc wrought on military objectives.

When we turn to the dirigible airship—the lighter-than-air machine—the comparison at first sight seems hopelessly against us. We have nothing that can be compared to the Zeppelin in either speed or power of destruction. We have, it is true, a number of airships of different types, but experience so far has not shown that they are of great, if of any, practical value. Our military authorities have deliberately pinned their faith to the aeroplane, and so far as this War is concerned it would appear that we are hopelessly outclassed in the matter of airships.

But we must not allow ourselves to be deceived by appearances. We must not fail to take into consideration the fact that so far as its real military value is concerned the Zeppelin has shown itself to be an absolute and costly failure. This may seem at first sight a hard saying when we think of the many victims of the Zeppelin raids, of the women and little children slaughtered, of the civilians murdered in midnight raids whose lives against any opponents with the slightest regard for the laws of war or for their own good name would have been absolutely safe.

But the facts cannot be disputed. The Zeppelin is a murder machine pure and simple. Its military value is absolutely negligible, and the destruction it has wrought has been of no military significance whatever. Out of all the victims it has claimed during its frequent nocturnal expeditions here and in France, only the barest handful have been soldiers, and on none of the raids has any military base sustained the slightest damage. Moreover, it has failed in its avowed object of terrorising; neither our own people nor the French have been weakened—rather have they been strengthened—in their determination to carry on the War to the only issue consistent with the future existence of civilisation. The only real and tangible results of the Zeppelin raids from a military point of view have been to cover the Germans with a stigma of crime and murder for which they will pay dearly in the future, and to make the Allies more than ever determined to root out the nest of vermin which for so long has troubled Europe. They have done more, perhaps, than anything else except the infamous submarine campaign to convince the civilised world that so long as Germany retains her power of mischief there will be no peace for the nations at large.

There is no disguising the fact, however, that, for what it is worth, the Zeppelin for the moment holds the field.

We have not yet succeeded in discovering any means either of keeping the raiders away when the conditions are favourable for their visits, or of dealing effectively with them when their presence is detected. Undoubtedly the problem is a very difficult one. Zeppelins can fly so high that gunfire is practically ineffective against them, as has been proved in the raids on both Paris and London; the one recently brought down by the French was flying much lower than usual. They are able to take very effective cover behind any clouds that may be about, and the difficulties by which the aeroplanes are faced in locating and attacking them at night appear to be well-nigh insuperable under present conditions. In time, perhaps, we shall have fleets of powerful aeroplanes which will be able to take the air and not merely rise swiftly to the height at which the Zeppelin flies, but remain aloft all night, if need be, until the dangers inseparable from a landing in the dark have disappeared.

But it must not be forgotten that the very factors which give the Zeppelin its invulnerability against attack practically destroy its value as a fighting machine. No one—not even the commanders of the Zeppelins themselves—would pretend that, flying at a height of 12,000 feet or so on a dark and cloudy night, they can say with certainty where they are, or that they can drop their murderous bombs with any sure hope of hitting an object which would be their justification from a military point of view. They simply wait until they think they are over an inhabited area, and then drop their bombs in the hope of killing as many people as possible, or, perhaps, luckily striking some material object and doing real damage. That is not war as the civilised world understands it, but simply anarchism.

A distinguished writer recently expressed the opinion that as the Germans were essentially a practical people they would not waste effort by dropping at haphazard bombs which they had been at such pains to carry to this country, and that they must therefore be genuinely under the impression that they were doing real military damage. But their whole record in the War entirely disposes of this theory. We know quite well—the Germans have told us so, and their acts have borne out their words—that the policy of "frightfulness" commends itself to their judgment. Their one idea is to terrify; they hope to do enough damage and kill enough people to bring about in England a movement for peace. Nothing but defeat will convince them that they are wrong.

And this consideration brings me naturally to another—the subject of reprisals. If we cannot stop the Zeppelins coming or deal with them adequately when they are here, can we teach the Germans a lesson which will convince them that two can play at the game of "frightfulness," and that in the long run we can play that game better than they can themselves? I think we can, and I think we should.

It has been one of the most striking characteristics of the career of Lord Rosebery that on more than one occasion he has put into terse and vigorous expression the opinions of the great majority of the English people. With all his apparent detachment, Lord Rosebery has a wonderful understanding of what England is saying, and still more what it is thinking, and the reader will call to mind more than one occasion on which the nebulous and only half-expressed thought of England has been suddenly crystallised in the clearest fashion through the mouth of Lord Rosebery. This has unmistakably been the case in the matter of the Zeppelin raids.

In a recent letter to *The Times*, dated February 3, Lord Rosebery put the English point of view with his customary clearness and directness. He wrote:

This last Zeppelin raid has cleared the air. There may be difficulties from the aircraft point of view in reprisals. I am not behind the scenes, and I do not know. But as regards policy there can be none. We have too long displayed a passive and excessive patience.

We all remember Grey's noble lines, "To scatter plenty o'er a smiling land." For "plenty" read "bombs" and you have the Prussian ideal. To scatter bombs over a countryside, to destroy indiscriminately the mansion and the cottage, the church and the school, to murder unoffending civilians, women, children, and sucklings in their beds—these are the noble aspirations of Prussian chivalry, acclaimed by their nation as deeds of merit and daring.

Let them realise their triumph. Let us bring it directly to their hearts and homes. Let us unsparingly mete out their measure to themselves. Nothing else will make them realise their glories. And the blood of any who may suffer will rest on their Government, not on ours.

I am firmly convinced that in that letter Lord Rosebery expressed not merely what the great mass of the English people are thinking and saying to-day, but that he expressed a great and real truth.

In the early days of the War it was the fashion here in England to affect to believe that we were at war not with the German people—represented by the pro-Germans in our midst as a kindly, harmless, and industrious lot of folks—but with the mysterious "military caste" who were supposed to have usurped all authority, and to be driving the delightful German people at large into the commission of all kinds of bestial outrages which were entirely foreign to their wholly delightful nature. I should imagine that fiction has long gone by the board. We have seen the "delightful" German nation sent into paroxysms of inhuman glee by such outrages as the sinking of the "Lusitania"; we have seen them time and again savagely gloating over the slaughter of men, women, and children by their murderous Zeppelins; and if those savage outbursts of delight have done nothing else, we have at least to thank them for teaching us the lesson that we are at war with the entire German nation, and that between that nation and the civilised world there is a great gulf fixed which in our time at least will not be bridged over.

Do we owe any consideration to such a nation? Do we owe to them any of the chivalry and honourable forbearance which we have shown, not once, but a thousand times, in our long contests with civilised adversaries on a hundred fields in all parts of the world? Are our hands to be tied and our people to suffer through our adherence to creeds of warfare which the Huns evidently regard—as they regard Christianity itself—as a lot of worn-out shibboleths?

I say emphatically "No," and I say the time has come when we should take steps, in Lord Rosebery's words, to bring home the triumphs of the Zeppelins to German hearts and German homes.

It is too much the fashion in this country to look upon the German as a stolid individual with nerves of steel, who is not to be shaken from his serenity by any of the trials which would bear hardly upon ordinary mortals. There never was a greater mistake. I am quite ready to admit that the German can look unmoved upon a great deal of suffering in other people—that is a characteristic of bullies of all nations; and if the German has not shown himself to be a super-man, he has at least convinced the world that he is the super-bully *in excelsis*. And the only argument that appeals to him is force, naked and unashamed. In his heart of hearts he knows it. That is why he believes that England to-day is cowering in impotent terror under the menace of the Zeppelins, because he knows that is exactly what he would be doing himself if the positions were reversed, and he cannot understand other people who are built on very different lines. We know how one of the early raids on Freiburg produced an instant panic flight of every German who could afford to get away from a district which had suddenly become "unhealthy."

Now we have it in our power to reproduce that panic in a dozen German towns within easy reach of our lines in France. And we know something of the real effects of a bombardment by one of the Allied squadrons. In the recent raid on Petrich only fourteen French aeroplanes took part. Yet the Bulgarians officially admitted that they sustained a thousand casualties—far more than we have suffered in the twenty odd Zeppelin raids on England.

Surely it is high time we made it clearly known that any repetition of the bombardment of an unfortified area would be followed by reprisals of the most merciless nature. We can imagine what the effect would be of a big British or French squadron of aeroplanes pelting the German frontier towns with a hail of high explosive and incendiary shells. Assuredly the Zeppelin raids on England would seem futile in comparison. And just as assuredly it would bring home to the German nation as nothing else ever will that the policy of "frightfulness" in which they have elected to indulge is one which will call down upon them a richly deserved punishment. I believe that, speaking generally, the entire world would approve of our action if we decided to take such measures of reprisals as German crimes call for. The responsibility would be Germany's, not ours. We have fought, as our French Allies have fought, with clean hands.

I believe that stern punishment of this nature is the only possible means of putting an end to the German campaign of murder, and it is for that reason that I advocate it without the slightest hesitation or compunction. The idea of those who believe that reprisals are called for is not to punish the Germans so much as to convince them of the error of their ways and to protect our own people. I believe that our air squadrons could set up such a reign of terror in the Rhine towns that even in Germany the demand for the only possible measure of protection—the cessation of the air raids on unfortified places in France and England—would become irresistible. The German Government may continue to delude the German people about events that are happening outside Germany; they could not by any possibility hide the facts if the air war were effectively carried on to German soil.

Further, I firmly believe that half a dozen smashing aerial attacks upon German towns and cities would do more to put a stop to Germany's unending infraction of all the laws of civilised warfare than the futile notes and protests of President Wilson have effected in a twelvemonth.

It will be objected by those who seek to make war in kid gloves that if we carry out these raids German women and children must inevitably suffer. I do not shrink from the conclusion, though I regret the necessity which has been forced upon us by the Germans themselves. I am not at all ashamed to say that one little English baby dead in the arms of its weeping mother, killed not by the accident of warfare, but of set, savage, and deliberate purpose, far outweighs in my mind any sentimental or humanitarian considerations for our enemies. We should have no ground of complaint if the Germans confined their raids to proper military objects; and if, in the course of those raids, civilians were accidentally killed, that would be one of the penalties of being at war, and we should be justified in asking our people to bear their sorrows with what fortitude they could. The case is widely different when men, women, and children are slain in a foul campaign of insensate murder; and I say again that in self-defence we are entitled to throw mere sentiment to the winds and protect ourselves by any means in our power. And the best means of protection we have against these murderous raids is to hit the Hun in the same way, to give him a taste of his own medicine; in the words of Lord Rosebery, to bring his triumph directly to his heart and his home. Thus, and thus only, we shall convince the German people, and through them the German militarists, that in the long last it does not pay to outrage the conscience of civilisation.

To sum up, I think it is certainly true to say that in the domain of the air the Allies have established and can maintain a definite superiority over the enemy. That they have established it is plain; that they can maintain it is, I think, equally plain, because they have the larger resources, and because successful aerial work calls for the exercise of qualities which both the French and the English possess in a far more marked degree than do the Germans. Our air raids have been far more destructive from the military point of view than anything the enemy has been able to accomplish; they have been better devised and more capably carried out by men who were better fitted for the task they had in hand. It remains to be seen whether the German superiority in the lighter-than-air machines will give them any real advantage.

At present all the arguments point to the greater value of the aeroplane upon which the Allies have pinned their faith. In any case, it is too late, probably, for us to take up the question of airship construction with any hope of making effective use of it during the present War, and we must do the best we can with what we believe to be the superior weapon. My own view is that on the whole the superiority of the Allies is fully assured, and that now and to the end the credit of winning the War in the air will and must remain with us.

Chapter Five
Britain's Unshakable Resolve

This War has brought many changes, and will bring many more. But it has brought one for which we cannot be too grateful, one which we may even think in the days to come was the justification and the reward for all the lives and all the treasure which the great struggle has demanded and will yet demand from us.

It has made of us one people. And when I say one people, I am not referring merely to the inhabitants of these small islands, which Britons all the world over will ever regard, as they have ever regarded, as "home." I include the great dominions over the seas—Australia, Canada, South Africa, New Zealand, and India, with their many races and many people who live and enjoy their lives under the benign shelter of the British flag.

Nothing the world has ever seen is equal in grandeur, and in the lesson it has taught us, to the majestic uprising of the British peoples when the first shock of war burst upon a startled world in those early days—how long ago they seem to-day!—of August, 1914. From the Tropics to the Poles not a dissentient voice was heard. It is not too much to say that the entire British Empire, which many of us had perhaps come to regard as somewhat a shadowy entity, leaped to arms with a unanimity which not only surprised us, but, as we have every reason to know, startled and bewildered our enemies.

Of our own people here at home we were always sure, provided they could be induced to realise the magnitude of the great struggle before them. Of that, from the earliest days of the violation of Belgium, there was never the slightest doubt. The British people are, and have always been, peculiarly sensitive to the sanctity of their pledged word; not for nothing have we earned the reputation that the Englishman's word is as good as his bond. And when our people realised that Germany, with a cynical disregard of international honour and good faith to which history happily offers few parallels, had deliberately attacked Belgium, there was at once an explosion of cold rage which, could the Germans but have understood it, would have convinced them that the British Empire was in this War, for good or ill, until a final settlement had been reached which would mean either absolute triumph or absolute annihilation.

We know, as a matter of fact, that England's decision to fight over a "scrap of paper" produced something akin to stupefaction in Berlin; we know also that it produced an outburst of hate which found its ultimate expression in the fatuous "Gott strafe England" which has become the by-word of the world as an expression of impotent rage and spite. We may take that as the greatest compliment an honest nation has ever received from a people to whom such a thing as honour and good faith is not only unknown, but is unimaginable. Knowing nothing of national honour themselves, the Germans were naturally unable to forecast accurately the course of action of either Belgium or Britain. From both of them they have received a much-needed lesson, which I have no doubt will be still further driven home by the stern logic of the events which are even now shaping dimly before our eyes.

It was just this consideration of national honour which brought not only England in particular, but the whole Empire, into the field as one man. Great armies sprang into existence before our very eyes. From every quarter of the globe offers of men, money, and supplies of all kinds were poured into our lap with a profusion which was as surprising as it was gratifying. We witnessed, in fact, what required a great national peril to bring to birth, the nascence of the British Empire as a fighting force. And anyone who fails to see that that fact will have a very profound influence upon the future history of the world must be blind indeed to the real significance of events.

The Empire has found itself. That is the one cardinal lesson which, above all others, stands out as the greatest feature of the world-war. Will anyone believe that Germany, with all the advantages she possesses in the matter of organisation and long preparation for war, could in the long last vanquish Britain, solidly united, armed to the teeth, her deficiencies at last made good, and ready to shed the last drop of her blood and spend her last shilling in defence of the glorious heritage which has been won in a thousand years of strife and struggle? If she stood alone to-day, without a single Ally in the world, Britain would never give up the struggle which has been thrust upon her. But she is not alone. She has powerful Allies who are as resolute as she is herself, who realise as fully as she does all that is implied in the threat of German domination, and who are as fully determined as she that "the Prussian ulcer" shall be cut once and for all from the body politic of civilisation.

Dealing for a moment with Great Britain alone, I do not hesitate to here say that our people are united in this great quarrel as they have never been united before.

In our other wars we have always had parties, more or less strong, but never negligible, which seemed to see in the enemy an object for friendship more attractive than our own people. We have always had parties which, if not openly, at least covertly, seemed to incline to the side of our foes. We all remember the South African campaign, when a very large and influential section of the Liberal Party went out of its way to champion the cause of Paul Kruger.

We do not need—and I have no desire—to dwell upon that unhappy time; many of those who then made a great mistake have to-day atoned for their error by their splendid efforts to vindicate the cause of Britain and civilisation in the present struggle. I mention the fact only to show that to-day there is no pro-German party in this country which carries the slightest weight. The pro-German element is conspicuous by its absence; it is represented only by a small rabble of discredited cranks and self-advertisers for whom the nation has shown its contempt in unmistakable fashion. The heart of the nation as a whole is sound, and it is firmly determined that Germany's eternal attempts to annoy and provoke her neighbours shall be once and for all suppressed.

I shall deal elsewhere with Germany's colossal blunders in regard to the War; I will content myself with saying here that her first and greatest mistake was in regard to the British Empire. She did not think we would fight, but if we did she thought there would be revolution in Ireland and India, and a sudden dropping off of our Colonial Dominions, leaving us so weak and so torn with internal dissensions that we should be in no shape to oppose her triumphal progress over the bodies of her enemies.

Over three million volunteers have rallied to the Colours in reply to the German challenge. Ireland to-day, dropping all her historic feuds, is practically solid for the Empire, and her sons, as ever, have shown their glorious deeds under the British flag. India, with one voice and heart, has rallied to the Empire; her men have given their blood without stint in our cause, her princes have poured out their treasure like water in our service, proud and glad to make what return they could for the blessings they have enjoyed under British rule. The deeds of the Canadians, the Australians, the New Zealanders, have added a new and imperishable tradition to British history. The bloodstained soil of the Gallipoli Peninsula will remain for all time hallowed by the glory of the men of Anzac, who, not once, but time and again, wrested seemingly impossible triumphs from the very jaws of death and defeat.

They failed, it is true, to win the last and greatest victory, but the story of their failure is more glorious than the story of many successes, and so long as our race and our language endure the tale of the landing at Suvla and the fight for the heights overlooking the Dardanelles will be told as an example of what human flesh and blood can achieve and endure. There is nothing greater or nobler in all our history; and while our Empire can produce such men as those who for long months faced the Turks in Gallipoli, we can be sure that in the British Empire the world will have a force to be reckoned with.

Turn to South Africa. There were those among us who felt after the Boer War that Britain was making a dangerous experiment in conferring absolute self-government upon those who but a short time before had been our implacable enemies. But the result was a triumph for British principles of liberty and of trust in the essential justice and equity of our rule. From the first, General Botha, our ablest and most chivalrous antagonist in the war, showed absolute and unshakable loyalty to the people who had put their trust in him. He was followed nobly by the great mass of the people of South Africa, Dutch as well as English; and when De Wet's misguided rebellion broke out it was suppressed with a swift efficiency which elicited unstinted admiration, not unmixed, it must be admitted, with surprise. Later we were to see the Union of South Africa playing a gallant part in the expulsion of German rule from the adjoining territories.

All this surely must have been a bitter pill for the Kaiser to swallow. We know how he encouraged Kruger in his revolt against the British; we know how confidently he had counted on disaffection in South Africa to add to our difficulties; we can imagine his joy when De Wet and his irreconcilables raised the standard of revolt, even though their motive was much more hostility to the English than love for the German.

We know he looked upon Ireland as hopelessly disloyal and ready to fling off for ever, perhaps with German help, the hated yoke of the Saxon. We know he looked upon India as seething with discontent and eager to fling herself into the arms of anyone who would give a hand in ejecting the brutal British Raj. We know he looked upon our Dominions as ripe fruit ready to drop off the parent tree at the slightest shake. We know he looked upon ourselves as a decadent nation, grown rich and indolent, caring for nothing but ease, and wrapped in a sloth from which we could never awaken until it was too late. And, lo! upon the first touch of war the weapons he had hoped to use shivered to fragments in his hand, the hopes he had fondly entertained turned to Dead Sea ashes in his mouth.

With one heart, one mind, and one unshakable purpose, the British Empire rushed to war. Swept away in an instant were those bad old party squabbles, those bad old party cries, with which our nation is prone to amuse itself in times of peace to the exclusion, perhaps, of more vital things. We seemed so desperately in earnest about our internal quarrels that perhaps we could not expect the continental nations, least of all the Germans, to realise that, for all our dispute, we are still one nation, that we are still animated by precisely the same spirit that has made England great, overlain though it may be by the dust and cobwebs that have grown up in a century of freedom from war on a great scale.

We do not perhaps quite understand ourselves; it would be certainly too much to expect the Germans to understand us, for they have shown an utter inability to understand any type of mentality but their own. Had they been better acquainted with our idiosyncrasies, I do not say that war would have been averted, but it would certainly have been postponed until Germany felt herself to be still stronger afloat and ashore, when the task of defeating her would have been even harder and more prolonged. So that perhaps we have reason to be thankful that, as the struggle had to come— and of that there cannot be the slightest doubt—it should have come early rather than late; we may have reason to be thankful, despite all the miseries and losses which the War has caused, that it was prematurely precipitated by German arrogance and greed and blindness. How much greater would have been her chances of success if she had been content to wait for, say, another five or ten years, when her prospects of meeting the British Fleet on something like equal terms would have been vastly improved!

And if our nation has closed its ranks and determined that this War shall be fought to the only finish consistent with the continued existence of civilisation as we understand it, what shall we say of our Allies? What tribute can be too great for the matchless heroism of France? How can we praise too highly the dogged courage of the Russian soldier, which has time and again saved the situation in the West by a display of self-sacrifice of which the world can offer few parallels?

What words can express all we owe to gallant little Serbia and Montenegro, crushed beneath the heel of the invader, yet destined to arise with their lustre undimmed and shining brighter than ever? How can we show our appreciation of what Belgium, the greatest martyr of all, has done for the sacred cause of liberty? Who can measure our debt to Italy, flinging herself into the great battle of freedom, not at a time when victory seemed assured, but when the clouds were thickest and our hopes at their lowest ebb?

Can we detect any sign of weakening in the Allies' stern resolve? Assuredly not. Bound together by a sacred pact to make no terms with the enemy which shall not be acceptable to all, they will go on from strength to strength, growing daily in power and resources, moved by one mind and by one purpose, till the time comes for the dealing of the last great blow which shall shatter finally and for ever Teutonic aspirations to rule the world. If signs of weakness there be—and they are not wanting—they are not to be found in the ranks of Germany's enemies. Rather are they to be found in the camp of the enemy himself. From all parts of the Teutonic Empires and their Allied nations come the signs which tell of war-weariness, of a growing conviction that further conquests are impossible, that the War has become a struggle for existence, that the enemy is knocking ever more and more loudly at the gate.

The scales are beginning to fall from the eyes of the German people. They are yet far from convinced that all is lost, but at least they are beginning to be sure that nothing is to be gained. No longer do we hear the boastful assertion that all their losses shall be made good by huge indemnities to be extracted from their crushed and beaten foes. A new note is being sounded of the need for sacrifice; new warnings are ever being given that Germany's war will have to be paid for by Germany, and not by the rest of the world. It is too early to say that German resolution is seriously weakened; it is not too soon to say that the German people are beginning to realise at last the strength of the combinations they have aroused against themselves.

On the other hand, the temper of the Allies, their confidence in their cause, and their ability to make that cause good has never stood so high. They have learned the lesson they needed eighteen months ago—that the War will be something far more serious and more terrible than they anticipated, that much remains to be done, that many sacrifices will have to be made before success crowns their efforts. But in learning that lesson they have also learned their own strength. They have learned, too, to trust one another, to see that the cause of one is the cause of all. And in the thoroughness with which they learn that lesson lies the strongest pledge for a happy issue. The Allies cannot be defeated so long as they remain true to themselves and to each other, so long as they remain bound together by the bonds of loyalty and constancy to a great and a sacred cause. That they are so bound to-day none can dispute; that they will remain so bound to the end it would be treason to them and to ourselves to doubt. Not to one but to each of the Allies in turn have the Germans gone with their insulting attempts to buy a separate peace, to achieve by sheer bribery what they have failed to achieve by force of arms in spite of all their "victories." By each of their opponents in turn they have been spurned with contempt. Russia simply tore up their clumsy tenders of treason without deigning even to reply. And, as we have since learned, even gallant little Belgium, torn and ravished as few countries have ever been torn and ravished in the world's history, spurned an offer which would have given her back much of what she had lost, but would have lost for her the priceless possession for which she fought—her national honour.

With these object-lessons before her eyes, perhaps in the days to come even Germany, who has shown herself so thoroughly oblivious to what honour and conscience mean, may realise that there are nations in the world to whom there are better and higher things than mere wealth and power, that there are principles which soar far above material considerations, that she is face to face with something which is at present far beyond her comprehension, and that something far mightier than the mightiest cannon ever forged in the furnaces of Krupps' is working for her downfall. That something is the moral sense of the world at large, of which, as yet, the Germans have not the slightest understanding. The German, even in the midst of his successes and triumphs, is faced by a resolution at least as great as his own, he is faced by men whose hearts are aflame with the sacred fire of liberty, he is faced by men to whom honour and good faith are all in all. And in the face of that combination even the boasted might and efficiency of Germany will go down at last, in the fullness of time, in hopeless and irretrievable ruin.

Chapter Six
The Terror in Germany

I am most emphatically not one of those who think we ought to take for granted all the stories we get, often from German sources, of the condition of things in Germany.

We know enough of German methods to know that for her own purposes she is capable of flying kites of varying types and shades; and one of the kites which was very prominently flown in the early days, comparatively speaking, of the War was the fiction that for her own brutal and illegal purposes England was "starving German babies" through the medium of her infamous (in German eyes) blockade.

It mattered nothing to the Germans that in 1871 the blockade of Paris and the starvation of the civilian people was one of the principal means by which she enforced the capitulation. The Hun never likes his own medicine. What was, when applied to France in 1871, a stroke of German genius, becomes, when applied by the British Fleet to Germany in 1915, a crime so infamous as to call down all the vengeance of heaven upon the brutal English.

In German eyes no weapon of war is legitimate if it is applied against the sacred persons of Germans; on the other hand, any and every device of the devil becomes a righteous punishment if it is used against Germany's enemies. Surely never was any people in the world so lacking in a sense of proportion and common sense! There is no doubt, I think, that the first "starvation" cries which emanated from Germany were a cunningly devised plan to work upon the sympathies of neutrals and, in particular, upon the United States. There are always in every country a certain number of good, sentimental souls whose hearts are apt to run away with their heads, who are apt to think or act very much as their emotions lead them, and are entirely incapable of looking at more than one side of any question. It was to just these people and, of course, to the German people in America, that the first frantic "starvation" appeals were directed. I firmly believe that at that time there was little or no serious shortage in Germany, and that the outcry that was raised was merely a ruse to catch the sentimentalists' attention.

It succeeded to a certain extent, and it gave the "hyphenated" section of the American people an opportunity of which they took full advantage for renewed girdings against England. But neither then nor at any other time did it succeed in its real purpose, which was to procure by fair means or foul a relaxation of the British blockade.

How serious that blockade was to become I do not believe the German people or the German rulers realised in the early days. I do not believe they realised that it was possible so completely to cut off their supplies as to produce anything like grave inconvenience, to say nothing of actual want. They have learned differently since! There is a growing volume of testimony from competent observers that the effectiveness of the British blockade is at last beginning to tell its story in Germany. The "bread cards," the "butter cards," the meatless days, the frantic appeals to the German people to give up the grease in which they love to bathe themselves at their meals, may be, as the Government pretends, merely a wise conservation of their resources. But if that is all, this "conservation of energy" is being carried out on a scale which is rapidly disheartening and discouraging the German people in every part of the Empire.

The following extract from a Copenhagen paper no doubt puts the case so high as to be practically a burlesque, but it at least shows that countries adjoining Germany, and in free communication with her, understand that the shortage of food and other supplies is far more serious than the Germans are prepared to admit. A Reuter telegram from Copenhagen says:

> The Labour journal, *Folkets Avis*, publishes a letter from a business man who has just returned from a six months' round tour of Germany, in which he describes the conditions there as more desperate than those in Paris in 1870. The writer is convinced that there is not now a living cat or dog in the whole of Germany, all having been eaten.
>
> Animal lovers trying to hide their pets have been betrayed by their neighbours and punished. Storks, swallows, starlings, and all kinds of wild birds have been systematically killed, and the result, he declares, will be felt in Scandinavian countries in the coming spring. All sea fowl have long since been exterminated.

I have not much doubt that this extract gives far too gloomy a picture if it is intended to represent the condition of the great mass of the German people; I do not believe, though I should like to, that starvation has gone so far as this. But it is more than likely—indeed, I believe it is practically certain—that there is in it a considerable basis of truth.

We have to remember that owing to the demoralisation of the German currency by the flood of paper money prices in Germany have gone up to an enormous extent, while at the same time, owing to the complete disappearance of her manufacturing and export business, wages have fallen in all but a few special trades. For this reason a large percentage of the population is feeling the pinch of want quite apart from any actual shortage of food in the country, and there may well be a good deal in the story of the Danish merchant that most of the wild birds, if not the very dogs and cats, have fallen victims to the necessity for obtaining food.

It will be convenient if we consider the shortage of necessaries in Germany under various heads, the first of which is naturally the deficiency in the food supply, since that is likely to exercise the profoundest influence on the great mass of the people. On this point we have abundant evidence, not only from neutrals who have been able to move more or less freely about Germany, but, still more important, from English people who have returned after being liberated by exchange or otherwise.

One and all are agreed that the German people are suffering from an actual shortage of food. It is not merely a question of prices, though these are far higher than they are in England, and the wealthy folk are still able to get almost all they want. There is, we are assured on evidence which it is practically impossible to ignore, a very serious shortage of many commodities of everyday use, the lack of which is severely felt, as, owing to the very high prices ruling, they are almost entirely beyond the reach of the people at large.

Now, in considering the question of the food supplies of Germany, it is important to remember that in normal times Germany imports some forty per cent, of the fodder used for feeding her sheep and cattle, and it is the scarcity of fodder that has produced the present shortage of meat. That such a shortage exists we know from the ordinances made by the German Government providing for two, three, and even four meatless days per week for everyone in Germany. In the early days of the War, confident that the struggle would be a short one, the Germans took no special pains to keep up their supply of cattle. It was only after the battle of Flanders that they discovered their mistake, and that the question of the supply of meat was destined to be critical.

Then came the panic legislation which led to the slaughtering of swine on an enormous scale. It was decided to devote all the available fodder to the feeding of cattle, since these would be the most difficult to replace after the War. Pigs were killed *en masse*, orders being given that the flesh was to be tinned to form a reserve. But it was soon found that even this was not sufficient to save the situation. Owing to the growing stringency of the blockade fodder for the cattle began to give out, and then it was decided to fatten pigs. In consequence the slaughter of cattle has increased enormously, and hence arises the growing shortage of milk, butter, and cheese.

Now whatever may be the leakages in the British blockade, it is quite certain that only the barest fraction of Germany's former imports is getting through; nothing can reach her directly oversea, and our trade agreements with neutral nations to prevent reshipment, even if they are not all that we could desire, are certainly having a very great effect. And it is certain that, despite smuggling on an unprecedented scale, Germany is very far from getting anything like all that she imperatively requires. The pinch is there, and it is growing, and that it is growing rapidly is shown by the increasing violence of the German threats against England and her incessant announcements that she is really getting ready for some new "frightfulness" that shall put all her previous efforts completely into the shade. We hear and note, but we are in no wise terrified.

Frantic efforts are being made by the Germans to purchase and import cattle food of all descriptions, and in addition such fats as butter, lard, and margarine, the shortage of which has produced an enormous effect throughout the Empire. It is our business to see that she fails; and with our Navy given a free hand, I am confident that we can do so.

We know how serious the shortage of bread has become; we know that no German can purchase bread without a "bread card," and that the amount he can purchase is severely restricted. We know that he is ordered not to eat meat on certain days of the week. We know, too, that in various towns, even in Berlin itself, the maddened people have already broken out into "bread riots," and that their mutinous gatherings have been dispersed by the police. Not even the well-drilled German will consent to go on indefinitely on an empty stomach. There have been cavalry charges in some towns, there have been violent riots in many, people have pillaged shops; "in fact," says the German writer of a letter found on a prisoner, "we have a war at home as well as abroad."

Another letter sent from Munich to "cheer up" a prisoner at Oleron says, "Wherever we go, and wherever we may be, we see nothing and hear nothing except misery and poverty." A letter from Greiben contains similar lamentations, and adds, "With all our strength we have accomplished nothing, and we shall soon be ruined."

Germany's chief imports at present, secured, of course, by devious ways since she is unable to import anything directly, are cotton, wool, copper, lead, paraffin, rubber, nickel, oils, wheat, rye, and barley. These are all of vital necessity to her continued existence, not merely to her successful conduct of the War. With the food shortage growing day by day, she must import even larger and larger quantities, and unless she can do so the end is inevitable; a point must come at which German moral will simply go to pieces. Our blockade is hastening that moment. None the less, we have to remember that starvation alone will not bring Germany to subjection; she will always obtain and grow supplies to a certain extent, probably enough to stave off actual starvation on a scale which would induce her to sue for peace. We have to complete the process of attrition, valuable as it is, by force of arms, and only a decisive military defeat will put an end to German aims and ambitions. That is a cardinal fact of which we must never lose sight.

There is hardly an article of food or drink for which the German chemists have not succeeded in finding more or less satisfactory substitutes. Bread is one of the best known instances. The German "kriegs-brod" or "war bread," though it is nothing like so palatable or so nourishing as ordinary bread, is yet sufficient to sustain life, though there is reason to think it sets up digestive disorders. Similarly, a glance at the German papers will show dozens of advertisements offering substitutes for endless other articles of diet. These substitutes are very interesting; whether they are satisfying is another question, and one which we can leave the beleaguered Germans to find out for themselves. "Acorn coffee," "artificial fats," "artificial honeys," wooden instead of leather shoes, "German tea" (whatever that may be), "egg substitute," "wood meal," sausage substitutes with "more than the nutritive qualities of beef"—these are only a few picked at random. No more convincing testimony to the value and effectiveness of the British blockade could be asked for. These are not the announcements of the German Government, intended to deceive, but the advertisements of business men who have to pay good solid German cash—or it may be notes!—for them. They speak more eloquently than any comment of ours could do.

A good deal of surprise has been expressed that, in view of the undoubted shortage of many necessities in Germany, there has been no apparent falling-off in the equipment or supplies of the German Army. In reality this is not a matter that need disturb our judgment on the general question. We have to remember that Germany is organised on a military basis, and that the militarist party, who most decidedly hold the upper hand, will see to it that as long as there is a pound of food in the country it will not be the Army that will go short. In every department of German life everything is subordinated to the demands of the Army, and no one can question that this is the correct policy. Any serious shortage or discontent in the Army would bring the military structure crashing to the ground, and there can be no doubt that the shortage which exists will have to go much farther before its effects are felt in the field. It will come, beyond doubt, but it is more than likely that shortage of men will make itself felt first.

The views of Abbé Wetterle on this point are worth quoting. He was before the War Deputy for Alsace in the Reichstag. When war broke out he escaped to France, and has lived there since. He considers that the Central Empires are already beaten.

> "Germany is at the end of her tether, that is the truth," he says. "She can no longer obtain credit, and the value of the mark is falling every day. After having mobilised ten million valid and invalid soldiers, Germany, whose losses number three and a half millions, and whose auxiliary services behind her lines require 1,700,000 men, can no longer fill the gaps in her Army, and her battle-line grows in extent every day. Famine stares her population in the face. By February or March at latest the lack of food will be severely felt. Riots have already taken place in her large cities, and they will gradually multiply and become more violent. Lack of men, lack of money, lack of food—such is the danger which threatens Germany."

Now we know very well that the German newspapers are controlled by the Government to an extent which is unknown in any other country in the world; not even the British censorship has such drastic powers. The columns of the German papers are therefore about the last place in which we should expect to find any inkling of the real situation as it exists in Germany to-day. It is the Government order that everything shall be painted *couleur de rose*. Yet even the German Press is becoming restive under the strain, and is beginning to say things which a very short time ago would have been impossible. Here is a telling extract from the Socialist paper *Vorwarts*, one of the few of the German journals which has risked a good deal in its insistence upon letting out at least some of the truth. It says:

> In a few weeks the sowing and preparing of the fields for the new harvest will have begun, and upon that harvest everything will depend. The coming harvest is of immeasurable importance for the German people. Fantastic speculations as to great imports of foodstuffs from the Orient have now become silent. Germany depends during the duration of the War upon her own production of food... It is evident now that our much praised organisation of our economic system is in no way so good as enthusiastic amateurs would like us to believe.

This is not exactly the language of a conquering nation whose Chancellor declares that she has sufficient for all her needs, but I have no doubt that it represents the real situation and reflects the prevailing anxiety much more accurately than Dr Helfferich's boasting speeches, which are undoubtedly meant for foreign consumption.

It is not merely in the matter of food supply that Germans are face to face with conditions which are giving her leading men cause "furiously to think." It is true it is what makes the most immediate impression on the public at large. But there are men in Germany who realise that there is a world to be faced when the War is over, and that as the days slip by Germany slips into a worse and worse position for meeting the conditions she will have to confront after the declaration of peace. I will first deal very briefly with some of the social aspects of Germany's present condition.

Germany's terrific losses in killed and maimed men, coupled with the terrible drop in the birth-rate, which has fallen far lower than it did in the Franco-Prussian War, are causing the gravest anxiety among the German economic thinkers. Next to the fall in the birth-rate, the rate of mortality among newly-born children is causing alarm; and when we remember how admirable are the German arrangements for the preservation of infant life, we can realise that very grave causes must be at work to account for the existing state of things. That those causes are connected in some degree with the efficacy of the blockade is probable, but a greater contributory cause has been the general distress caused by the War, and the failure of the municipal authorities to provide the necessary relief.

The pensions payable to the widows of German soldiers who have died in action are very small; distress and misery have entered the families where there are many children, and many of those are succumbing to the prevailing lack of food. To such a pitch has Germany been brought by the insane ambition of her rulers!

Orphans in Germany now number 800,000, Many of these orphans must for years remain a tax upon the State; they will be *bouches inutiles* until they reach the wage-earning age, and they will provide after the War, just as they are providing at present, a problem which will tax Germany's economic and administrative resources to the uttermost.

Another problem with which the Germans will have to deal is the appalling increase in crime. In spite of the fact that a great proportion of the men of the country are serving with the Army, the statistics of crime make appalling reading, and offences of all kinds are especially numerous among children. The juvenile Hun behaves as a Hun to the manner born once he is removed from the stern parental control which in times of peace keeps him within what, for Germany, are reasonable bounds. And even in times of peace the figures of juvenile crime in Germany are terrible. In the year 1912 the following crimes were committed in Germany by boys between the ages of twelve and eighteen:

> Criminal assaults, 952.
> Murder and manslaughter, 107.
> Bodily injuries, 8978.
> Damages to property, 2938.

These figures *for boys alone* are far more than the entire total of such crimes ever committed in England. For instance, the yearly average of crimes of malicious and felonious wounding in England for the ten years 1900-1910 was 1,262; in Germany for the ten years 1897-1907 it was 172,153. And the population of Germany may be taken at 65,000,000, with that of England at 45,000,000. These statistics give us some idea of the real character of the nation which holds itself up as the apostle of "kultur" to the rest of the world, and shows us what blessings we might expect under Teutonic rule.

It is naturally very difficult to get thoroughly reliable information as to the exact condition of things in Germany. Most of the "neutrals" whose stories appear in the English Press appear to be rather too apt to say the things which they think will best please English readers. None the less, their stories cannot all be invented, and we have valuable corroboration of many of them in the shape of reports published by neutral observers in the neutral Press—especially in countries where the prevailing sympathy tends to be pro-German—and from our own people who have returned from Germany.

A particularly valuable example of the former comes from Copenhagen. Dr Halvdan Koht, one of the foremost Norwegian historians, is known for his distinctly pro-German leanings. Yet, after a prolonged stay in Germany, he draws in the Christiania newspaper *Social Demokraien* a decidedly dismal picture of German life and of the state of public feeling in Germany. "The people are tired of the War" is his conclusion. It is true the whole country considers that Germany is safe, but the whole country has arrived at the conclusion that its adversaries, especially Great Britain, cannot be crushed. The fact that Great Britain is still in full possession of all her territories, that she cannot be attacked on land, and is less affected by the War than Germany is rapidly dawning on the whole people. Moreover, it is being realised that, in spite of her immense military strength, Germany will never be able to enforce a definite decision in her favour. Dr Koht interviewed a number of people of all classes on this subject, and all expressed similar views and heartfelt weariness of the War.

On this subject I might also quote the view expressed by a lady who reached England recently, one of the first batch of the so-called "reprisal women" who, the Berlin authorities have decided, are eating too much meat and butter, and must therefore be sent home. "Germans are suffering agonies," this lady said, "especially the poor people. They know, in spite of the lying Press, that their sufferings are merely beginning, and they are preparing themselves for more suffering until their rulers are forced to realise that the limits of endurance have been reached, and then sue for peace." The Germans, she added, "are ready to bear the financial losses and the appalling losses in men, but life on rations is simply driving them insane. The bread cards at first amused them like children, as one more opportunity of obeying orders, of which they are so fond. Now they have butter cards, fat cards, and, in some places, petroleum cards."

I do not think we can disregard all the evidence that is rapidly accumulating as to the widespread distress in Germany to-day. And I do not think that that distress is likely to decrease. We have it on the authority of Mr Asquith that the tightening of the blockade is proceeding, and the tighter we pull the strangling knot which the British Navy has drawn round the German neck, the sooner we shall return to the days of peace.

But, in the words of Lord Headley, "When Germany wobbles we must hit as hard as possible in the right place and in the right way. But let us make sure of our own set purpose and fixed resolve, that now that we have made up our minds, there shall be no indications of wobbling on our part." That, I think, expresses the judgment of the nation as a whole. We do not want to sit down in the hope that the "war of attrition" will do our business for us. It is "the long push, the strong push, and the push all together" of Britain and her Allies which alone will bring us to a triumphant success. The "war of attrition" is helping to bring nearer the day when the great push will be possible, but of itself alone it will never compel victory over an enemy who—it would be foolish to think otherwise—will fight to the last gasp.

Chapter Seven
Germany's Bankrupt Future

I have no hesitation in saying that from our point of view one of the most encouraging features of the whole situation is the extraordinary collapse of German credit—extraordinary, I mean, in comparison with her apparent successes in the campaign on land. The heavy decline in the value of German and Austrian money in neutral countries is an absolutely unmistakable sign that the finances of our enemies are, after eighteen months of War, reaching a condition which before long must prove a source of the gravest embarrassment to the Central Powers.

As I write, the exchange value of the sovereign in the United States is about two per cent, below normal, and the same condition exists in Holland and Scandinavia. Considering how much we have been buying abroad, such a trifling depreciation in our credit is a wonderful testimony to the stability of British institutions. But if we turn to German and Austrian currency we find that it has declined in value from twenty to thirty per cent. In other words, neutral countries are beginning to show themselves unwilling to take German money; and as Germany can now buy only from neutral countries, it is quite obvious that she not only has a difficulty in paying for her purchases, but that she has also to pay an exceedingly inflated price for them.

My readers will remember the sensation that was caused when, owing to our heavy purchases of food and war material from America, the value of the sovereign dropped something like six per cent. That meant that for every hundred pounds we paid to America for goods bought we were losing six pounds owing to the fall in the exchange; and when it is recalled that our purchases were on a scale which involved hundreds of millions, it will be seen that the decline was a very serious matter for us. But so good was our credit that there was no difficulty in floating a huge loan in America, and the result was that the value of the sovereign at once appreciated, and it has never seriously dropped since; in fact, it has steadily risen. The process was helped by selling American securities, of which we hold huge sums. We can repeat both processes as often as we like in reason, because our credit is good, and our holdings of American securities are still enormous. Germany can do neither—firstly, because her credit is utterly impoverished, and, secondly, because, whatever she may sell, she and those with whom she would like to deal have no security that the goods would have more than a very slender chance of getting through the British blockade. Here, again, we see how our overwhelming sea power is helping the cause of the Allies. In spite of the huge sums we are spending, Germany is infinitely worse off than we are, and there is every reason to believe that the tremendous fall which her money is now experiencing means that her credit abroad is rapidly nearing the exhaustion point.

The fall in the value of German money tends to show that our blockade is operating with increasing stringency and success. It seems probable enough that Germany can still manage to obtain through the neutral countries many of the things of which she has most pressing need. But apparently her export trade has been much more severely hit. She depends for this trade upon the import of raw materials, most of which are extremely bulky and quite unlikely to escape the unremitting vigilance of the British Navy. Consequently Germany finds herself unable to pay for her imports by the ordinary channels of international trade, and the difficulty of paying at all has become serious. Nearly all modern business is done on a paper basis; that is to say, on promises to pay—in other words, on credit—and credit obviously depends upon the financial stability of the concern or the nation which seeks thus to obtain goods. That is why the continued decline in the value of the paper mark shows the declining confidence of the neutral nations in Germany's power to redeem her pledges when the time for payment comes. Germany's ultimate solvency depends upon her ultimate victory, and we can see by the reluctance of the neutral nations to give credit to Germany that they are very far from satisfied with Germany's prospect of coming out "on top." And when neutral financiers come to the conclusion that the War will end in Germany's absolute bankruptcy—that is, in her inability to pay more than a few shillings in the pound of her debts—the value of her paper promises will sink almost to vanishing point, and there will be such a financial crash as this world has never seen. The faith of the neutral in German stability is wavering already, while the Allies still hold the confidence of the world. That is a factor of supreme importance. The day will come when not a single neutral will trade with Germany except on a gold basis, and when that day dawns the utter collapse of the Central Powers will assuredly be close at hand.

We have just seen a very striking evidence of Germany's impoverishment in regard to the supply of wheat which Germany desired to purchase from Rumania. If there is one commodity which Germany needs more than any other to-day it is wheat. Rumania demanded that the wheat should be paid for in gold in Bucharest. The German and Austrian Governments offered anything and everything else except gold. They offered first ammunition, then paper, then Rumanian Treasury bonds, ammunition, and paper. The Rumanians, however, insisted upon gold, and the deal fell through for the simple reason that Germany had no gold to spare. Few instances have been more eloquent of the state to which Germany is reduced. And what Rumania says to-day the rest of the neutrals are likely enough to say to-morrow—"Either gold or no goods." We can be quite sure that if Germany meets with a single great defeat in the operations which are assuredly near at hand, there will be a revulsion of feeling in the neutral countries which will render the demand for gold insistent. And if Germany cannot find gold to pay for the wheat she so sorely needs from Rumania, what are her prospects of finding it for other countries?

Now the German method of financing the War has constituted one of the most extraordinary gambles known in the history of finance. She has piled up an enormous debt in paper. The *Economist* estimates the total of Germany's war credits up to the end of December last at 1,500 million pounds sterling, and the average monthly war expenditure at 92.350 million pounds. Towards this Germany had raised up to September 15, 1915, 1,280 million pounds. In Germany these loans have been cited as a proof that financially the country is impregnable. But this assertion does not convince. The loans have been obtained only by wholesale inflation through borrowing on Treasury bills from the Reichsbank. The amount of these bills outstanding is carefully concealed from the world, but it is certainly enormous, and it seems to be rising rapidly again, though Germany's third loan was floated quite recently. The amount of these bills on January 15 was estimated at 250 million pounds. It is easier to trace the amount of the inflation of the currency by paper, and by paper without any gold backing. Between July, 1914, and January 15, 1916, the amount of Reichsbank notes in circulation increased from 95 million pounds to 319 million pounds and the amount of Treasury notes from 7 million pounds to 16 million pounds, while another 54 million pounds in paper was added in the form of Loan Office notes. That is to say, since the outbreak of war the amount of paper currency has increased from 101 million pounds to 389 million pounds, or about 285 per cent. How much the financial position has been worsened by the extension of banking credits we do not know, as the bi-monthly statements of the great banks have, most significantly, been discontinued. It is true that during the same period the amount of gold in the Reichsbank has been increased by 55 million pounds. But a large part of this increase, it is believed, came from the reserve of the Austro-Hungarian Bank, and in any case it is not nearly sufficient to have the smallest effect in counteracting the flood of paper. The effects of the inflation of the currency and its debasement by the huge issues of paper money are seen in the rapid collapse of the mark and the equally rapid rise in prices which in Germany to-day is making the lives of the poorer people well-nigh unbearable. And it is most noteworthy that in those countries where Germany has been able to trade with the greatest freedom the collapse of German credit is most unmistakable. That is for Germany, as well as for ourselves, a grave and unmistakable fact; it is verily the writing on the wall. Germany has been weighed and found wanting in the balance of the neutral nations who are more friendly disposed towards her.

To meet the expense of the War Germany has issued paper to her own population on a scale of which the world has had no experience. In return for the paper promises of the Government they have poured out with a lavish hand everything of which the Government stood in need, and it is impossible not to marvel at what is either patriotism or a very high order of gullibility carried to the extremest limits. In either case Germany's people have lent to her vast sums for a mere paper security, quite apart from the amounts she has expended in other countries and which she will have to pay for in gold or exports, which come to the same thing. What, we may well ask, will be the position when, after the War, German merchants want money—not paper—to resume their trading with the rest of the world, to purchase the raw material upon which the very life of her commerce depends? How is the Government to raise the gigantic sums that will be required not merely to pay interest on this stupendous pile of debt, but to begin to form a sinking fund to pay it off?

My own view—and it is shared by many others—is that Germany's borrowings on such a stupendous scale were made possible only because the German people, convinced that they were really and truly the supermen they fancied themselves to be, were firmly persuaded that they were going to win the War "hands down." They were assured *ad nauseam* that speedy victory was certain, that France was to be instantly crushed and Russia crippled, that Britain could not intervene in anything like decisive fashion in time to save her Allies, and that the end of the War would come in a few months at most, with a triumphant Germany extorting untold millions in the shape of indemnities from her trampled and bleeding enemies. The War was to be, in fact, a highly profitable trade undertaking, in which Germany's losses in killed and maimed were to be more than compensated for by increased wealth drawn from the coffers of her enemies, and especially England, the worst enemy of all.

But the War has not quite "panned out" to schedule, and Germany is to-day rapidly realising the fact. "In my opinion," said Lord Inchcape, speaking at the annual meeting of the National Provincial Bank of England,

"Germany is already irretrievably beaten, and no one knows this better than she does herself." That is a very strong expression of opinion from a man who is in a position to know what he speaks of when he deals with matters of finance. As I have said before, I do not believe that money alone can win the War, but there can be no reasonable doubt that the growing financial difficulties of Germany are swiftly bringing her to a position in which she will find it impossible to oppose with any hope of success the steadily growing power of the Allies. So much at least money can do and is doing, though the final blow must be dealt in decisive military action. Otherwise Germany will never be convinced that she is really and truly beaten, her people will be told again that they are unconquerable, and she will begin with all her wonderful organising powers to prepare for a renewed campaign of aggression in the future.

I cannot see how Germany is to be preserved from national bankruptcy; I cannot conceive any means by which she can hope to pay off the enormous debt she has piled up. Her export trade is utterly smashed, and it must take years to get it back even if the Allies are foolish enough after the War to allow her the commercial privileges she has enjoyed in the past, which is most unlikely. Her losses in men and material have been stupendous, she is eating herself up, she is blazing away her piled-up wealth at a time when she cannot keep going even a fraction of her commerce to make up for the steady drain upon her. We at least are free to trade overseas to as great an extent as we can manufacture, and it is a very gratifying fact that the trade of the United Kingdom has in the past few months shown a steady increase; February showed an advance of 10 million pounds on the corresponding month of 1915. We are not losing our markets to the extent that Germany is, for the simple reason, again, that our Fleet can keep open our trade routes. And we have also to pay regard to the fact that the German is not going to be a popular individual for a good many years to come in any civilised country. At the best he is going to have a good deal of trouble to persuade any of the Allies to do business with him on any terms whatever; at the worst it is more than likely that he will find himself shut out completely by an overwhelming tariff from every British, French, Russian, Italian, and Japanese market. How, under such conditions, Germany will ever succeed in paying her debts I cannot understand.

Borrowing in such a War as this is unavoidable for any of the belligerents; it is impossible to defray the stupendous cost out of income. The whole problem to be solved is whether it is possible to secure by taxation the interest on the increased debts and also a margin of revenue which during the War will help to pay for it, and after the War will provide a sinking fund to gradually pay off the sums borrowed. Germany's paper system is all wrong, because, in the first place, she has not the gold to back it up, and, in the second place, because no provision has been made by taxation to raise sums sufficient to provide interest and sinking fund. Even before the War Germany's yearly budgets have been showing a series of deficits, and with the stupendous amount she has added to her debts it is difficult to see how after the War is over she will be able to avoid defaulting. She will certainly not succeed in securing any indemnity as she did from France in 1871; she will far more probably find herself condemned to pay at least sufficient money to provide for the rehabilitation, so far as is possible, of Belgium.

There is, it is true, one aspect of the case which is to some extent favourable to Germany. A great portion of her war debt—in fact, practically the whole of it—is held at home, and it is quite possible that at the end of the War the people who have entrusted her with their savings will find themselves told that they will have to wait indefinitely for their money. Repudiation on this scale would perhaps enable Germany to keep herself right with the rest of the world and avoid actual default in the international sense. But the effect on her own people would be appalling! Now it is a very remarkable fact that though the German Government has carefully kept from the mass of the people any real knowledge of the facts of the situation as we know it exists, it has during the past few months been allowing certain newspapers to warn the public in guarded terms of what is coming. The *Berliner Post* states openly that the situation is "terrifying." That is a good deal of an admission for a people who a few months ago were setting out, as they themselves said, on a conquest of the world, and were going to extort the cost from their beaten enemies. Warning the German people that they must be prepared for very bad times, the *Post* goes on to say:

> Even the highest war indemnity that is thinkable cannot preserve us from a stupendous addition to the Imperial Budget for 1916-17. Without war damages we shall have to reckon upon an increase in the yearly taxation of at least four milliards of marks. From a technical point of view alone such amount cannot be procured immediately by taxation. From the political point of view it would be a great mistake if the population was not gradually acquainted with the situation, which, looked upon as a whole, has something terrifying about it.
>
> Only by slowly being made accustomed to it can the situation become softened for the people. Probably the State Secretary for Finance, when he introduces his proposals for the new taxation, will give as near as possible a review of what the

annual deficit will be. German people will only then be able to understand what wounds the War has made and what great measures will be necessary for years to come to heal them. At present the greatest part of the people probably has no idea of the situation.

It is perhaps permissible to ask, in view of this outburst, what the German people, deluded and hoodwinked for so long, are likely to say when the full facts break upon their minds. It will be noted that the *Berliner Post* deals with the financial situation apart from the war expenses, and finds very little comfort in it. The German people will find still less to be exultant about when the whole truth appears, as sooner or later it must, for it cannot be hidden much longer. Up to the present Germany has imposed practically no new taxes; they will be on a crushing scale when the German people have to set themselves to pay the damages involved in the conflagration which they so wantonly provoked.

But, doubters will ask, are we in any better case? I will quote in answer Sir George Paish, one of our leading financial authorities. "We may confidently expect," he recently declared, "that the nation after the War will have as much capital for investment as before the War."

In twelve months of war Great Britain has been able to buy and to pay for nearly 900 million pounds of Colonial and foreign produce and goods for home consumption and for war purposes. In addition she has found something like 350 million pounds of money for her Allies, Colonies, and customers. She has met her own war expenses, amounting to 1,000 million pounds, exclusive of the 350 million pounds supplied to her Allies and Colonies for war purposes. This great amount of money has been found with surprising ease. But it is during the current year that we shall feel the severest strain. We have to maintain upon the seas a Fleet even more powerful than that of last year, to provide our Allies, Colonies, and friends with at least 400 million pounds in loans, and to support in the field forces numbering nearly four million men, which will cost anything up to 2,000 million pounds. And in spite of these gigantic liabilities we find to-day that British credit stands practically unimpaired, while that of Germany is rapidly falling, and may soon vanish altogether. If the War has done nothing else, it has given the world such an example of financial stability as has never been seen.

It is the deliberate opinion of Sir George Paish that our position after the War will be just about where we stood at the beginning. We shall have sold a great many of our foreign securities, but, on the other hand, we shall have bought others from our Allies, customers, and Colonies, and, on balance, neither our home nor our foreign wealth will have been appreciably reduced. What we shall have lost will be our new savings. This loss amounts already to about 600 million pounds; if the War lasts another year it will have reached 1,000 million pounds in comparison with what our wealth would have been but for the War.

Of course, we shall have created a great debt. Already our debt, including the pre-war debt, is about 2,200 million pounds, and the debt charge and current Government expenses are about 300 million pounds. But it must be remembered that some 100 million pounds of this is interest which accrues to British investors, and that a large part of this interest will still be available for new capital purposes. Our losses in men will be grievous. But it must be recalled that one lesson of the War is that the whole nation is learning to work harder and more efficiently and that, in consequence, it is very doubtful whether our productive capacity has been seriously, if at all, reduced. When our men return from the War we shall have an enormous supply of labour available, and for the full employment of that labour we shall be able to find the capital. Will Germany be in anything like so favourable a position?

The bold and courageous policy of Mr McKenna in grappling adequately with the problem of finance has secured the emphatic approval of the entire nation. New burdens have been cheerfully shouldered; the country has shown unmistakably that it is prepared to make any sacrifices to win the War, and we have seen the income-tax doubled with far less protest than would have been aroused by the addition of a penny a few years ago. The nation has set itself to meet the cost of the War in the only possible way, by reducing all unnecessary expenditure, public and private, and devoting itself to the maintenance of our essential services, anxious only that so long as efficiency is secured money shall not be spared. We have boldly faced the enormous additional taxation rendered necessary by the gigantic war expenditure, and therein we have a tremendous advantage over Germany, who is only now beginning to consider the new taxes that will be required, and does not seem particularly gratified by the prospect with which she finds herself faced. Ominous mutterings of the coming storm are already to be heard, and when that storm breaks not even the iron discipline with which the Prussians have dragooned the entire German people will suffice to protect them from the wrath of those whom they have so grossly deceived. I do not know whether the German Government will dare to attempt to impose anything like the taxation which would be necessary to make provision for the war debt, but I am at least certain that as matters stand in Germany to-day the people have neither the will nor the ability to find the money. They have been fed with lying assurances that the money is to be found by someone else, and their rage and disappointment when they find out how they have been deceived will, beyond doubt, lead to consequences little foreseen by the light-hearted blunderers who set half the world in flames eighteen months ago.

I do not think that either now or in the future we need fear any comparison between the financial position of Britain and of her enemy. We are, and always have been, a far wealthier nation than the Germans; our credit is good, while Germany's is tottering to complete collapse; our resources in capital are as yet not seriously touched; our trade, even though its volume be diminished by the withdrawal of men for the Army and for munition making, still goes on as far as we can carry it. The real financial strength of the British Empire has as yet not been fully marshalled for the fray, and should the day ever come when money must be found beyond the resources of ordinary taxation there are vast reservoirs of strength which will yield supplies in abundance. For we are in this War to win—let there be no mistake about that—and to gain a complete and lasting victory there is no sacrifice that our people, properly instructed, will refuse to make. "To the last man and the last shilling" if necessary must be our motto. Our people ask only for a definite and a strong lead; if they get that, we need have no fear of the outcome of the greatest struggle we have ever been called upon to wage.

Chapter Eight
The Invisible Hand

I may fairly claim to have taken perhaps a leading part in bringing home to the people of this country a realisation of the perils to which our foolish good nature has exposed us in the matter of the spy danger.

Though I am quite willing to admit that much has been done by our excelled Intelligence Department in putting a check upon the activities of the German spies since the War began, I cannot but confess that I look upon the continued presence in this country of some 22,000 German and Austrian enemies, allowed for the most part to go freely about their business, whatever it may be, with unmixed alarm.

I raised my voice against the presence of spies among us before the War, and since. Indeed, since the outbreak of hostilities I have addressed over a hundred audiences upon this very vital aspect of the War.

Before the crisis—as long ago as 1906—I wrote and spoke of German spies; but for my pains I was jeered at by the public, laughed at by officialdom, and boycotted by a section of what is to-day known as the "Hush-a-bye Press." Many times I sat with Lord Roberts, both of us in a state of despondency. He had tried to do his best to awaken Britain and point out the pitfall ahead, and I had, in my own modest way, endeavoured to assist him. But it was all to no purpose; and when I wrote the forecast, *The Invasion*, to which Lord Roberts wrote a striking preface, people busy with their money-making and under the hypnotism of the Hun, declared that the great Field Marshal was "old," and that I was a mere "alarmist."

In this War, united as we are to-day in the common cause, we have buried the past. The future alone—the way to win the War—concerns us.

We know quite well, and the facts have been admitted since the War began, that in times of peace not only our own country, but practically every country in the world, was overrun with a horde of Germans who, though ostensibly in business on their own account, were, in fact, secret agents for that department known as "Number 70, Berlin." No nation has ever carried espionage to such lengths as it has been carried by the Germans, perhaps because there is no nation capable of so shamelessly abusing the hospitality of others and so flagrantly returning evil for good. I have no doubt whatever that the laxity shown not only by ourselves, but by other nations to Germans in times of peace, has been a matter for unmixed amusement in the secret councils of the Kaiser at Potsdam. To live in apparent peace and friendship for the express purpose of betraying is a Judas-like achievement in which no nation but the barbaric Teuton could take a pride, and there is ample evidence that before the War this was one of the favourite methods by which the German abroad served the interests of the Fatherland. This I have pointed out for years.

It cannot, alas, be pretended that, even since the War began, we have taken anything like adequate steps to protect ourselves against this grave national peril. Upon the outbreak of the War Germany took steps at once to intern or expel every enemy alien, and thus to put them out of the way of doing any injury. We cannot and do not complain of this; the complaints that have been made against the German proceedings were on the ground that the people interned were treated more like beasts than human beings. The mere fact of expulsion or internment was a matter of ordinary prudence, and the Germans were unquestionably right in taking no chances in the matter of espionage. Their action was only another instance of the thoroughness with which they had prepared for war, for there is no doubt that the steps taken were resolved upon long before war broke out; they could not otherwise have been taken with such promptness and on so great a scale.

Have we been as prudent? What was our action? Of the facts with regard to German spies in England the Government had been fully warned long before the War, and there was and is no excuse for any shilly-shallying with the subject. Yet for a long period hardly any action was taken to prevent the continued existence of a great danger, and it was only when the population became dangerously excited after the sinking of the "Lusitania" that internment was taken in hand with anything like vigour. And even this promise of Mr McKenna's has not been maintained, for we are now informed officially that there are still some 22,000 Germans and Austrians uninterned! Can it be said that these people do not constitute a very grave and a very real danger?

I am quite willing to admit that a proportion of them are perfectly respectable, honest folk who have no sympathy, it may be, with the cause of Germany, and who would not do anything to harm the country of their adoption. There are undoubtedly even Germans who are not devoid of all decent feeling. But there can be little question that a great many of them are of quite another way of thinking, and would be only too willing to commit outrage, wreck trains, blow up factories, destroy munition works, and stab us in the back if the opportunity offered itself.

Some months after the War broke out Mr McKenna, who was then Home Secretary, published a long report in which he dealt with the steps that had been taken to break up the German spy system in England. Possibly the then existing spy organisation was very badly crippled—perhaps for a time it was even destroyed. But the Germans are a pertinacious people; they have since had time to reorganise and perfect their plans, and I have no doubt they have done so. That we have interfered with them is unquestionable, and thanks to the increasingly stringent passport system—adopted shortly after it was advocated in my book *German Spies in England*—the German agents no doubt find it increasingly difficult to come and go undetected. It has, however, to be recognised that no passport system can keep these gentry out altogether; we know that even in France the German agents, whether actually Germans by birth or not, are very active. We know, too, that they are active here; we have caught and shot no fewer than ten of them up to the time of writing. But will it be pretended that we have caught them all? It is much more likely that many of them are still at large among us, and still active, though their opportunities for mischief have been very drastically restricted by the admittedly splendid work of our Naval and Military Intelligence Departments.

Now I think it will be admitted that the purpose of internment is not punitive, but preventive. We do not want to visit the misdeeds of Germany upon those Germans who are helpless in our midst; we do not want to inflict any unnecessary hardships on those who are not in a position to defend themselves, and who, whatever their nationality, cannot be held responsible for the bestiality which has made the name "German" accursed for ever among civilised nations. But we do want, and I maintain that we are entitled, to protect ourselves against those who, living here unmolested, are eager to return only evil for good. If in the course of protecting ourselves we inflict some hardships on those who do not deserve them, we can feel regret, but we cannot blame ourselves. The fault lies not with us, but with those who plotted and arranged for war on an unexampled scale, and whose proceedings before and after war broke out were of a kind which put them completely out of court if they plead for any kind of consideration.

Without hesitation I say that it would be practically impossible for a German spy to do any effective work here if he were not aided and abetted by Germans resident in England. To be of any real value a spy must have been trained as such, and he must have a base from which to work; he must have a shelter in which he will be practically free from suspicion; he must have messengers and go-betweens who can move about freely without attracting undue attention. And it is quite certain that no German spy coming to England can obtain all these things except with the active help of

Germans already domiciled here—naturalised Germans who are enjoying absolute freedom.

More than one German prisoner has escaped from our internment camps under circumstances which suggest very strongly that he has received help from people outside. That those people were British I refuse to believe. The inference is that they were Germans, and the conclusion is that all such people ought either to be interned or bundled, bag and baggage, out of the country. There is no safety in any middle course. It is for these reasons that I do urge very strongly that the Government shall at once take steps to see that all enemy aliens shall either be expelled or interned. I am convinced that our apathy in this direction, though it springs from feelings which are in every way creditable to our hearts, if not to our brains, is exposing us to dangers which, in these critical days, we should not be called upon to face.

The activity of German spies in England at the present moment needs no demonstrating. The Government has admitted it by the drastic steps they have taken to deal with the peril. But every nation spies during wartime, whatever they may do in peace, and I am certainly not going to blame the Government because German agents are able to come over here and send home information which may be of value to their country. Probably it would not be possible for the Government to stop them coming, and our Intelligence Department is entitled to congratulations upon the excellent work that has been done in detecting them. When the full story of their activities is told—if it ever is—it will be found how we have very often met and beaten the Hun at a game which he has been apt to consider as peculiarly his own. At the same time I do not think we have done all that we could and should have done, and the readiest way of helping on the good work would be to remorselessly intern or expel all enemy aliens, no matter what their status may be.

I am convinced that we should thus deal a formidable blow at the activities of the spies who visit our shores from time to time. They would be deprived at a stroke of their best protectors, and they would be exposed to a very greatly increased risk of detection. I admit that it would be very regrettable if some thousands of innocent Germans and Austrians, who, it may be, have a genuine admiration for England, and many of whom have sons serving in our Army, were thus inconvenienced. But the plain fact is that we cannot afford to take a single unnecessary risk, and whatever may be the inconvenience to the individual the safety of the State must be the first consideration.

It has been shown over and over again, both here and in other countries, that naturalisation is one of the favourite devices of the spy. It protects him by rendering him less likely to suspicion, and enables him to move about freely in places where the non-naturalised alien would have no chance of going. It has been proved during the present War that German troops have been led by men who had actually lived for many years in the district, and had come to be looked upon almost as natives. Naturally they made exceedingly efficient guides. Yet under cover of naturalisation they had been able for years to carry on active espionage work.

Then we also have the Invisible Hand. From August, 1914, to the present day a mysterious, silent, intelligent, Anglo-phobic mailed fist has been steadily at work for our discomfiture. Evidence of the existence of the Invisible Hand lies broadcast. As far as I know, however, only one person has publicly referred to it—the brilliant and well-informed writer who chooses to be known as "Vanoc," of the *Referee*.

He has pointed out that no effort has been made to locate, to destroy, or to intern the owner of the Invisible Hand. Yet we have seen its deadly finger-prints in many departments and in many parts of England, Scotland, and Wales. We recognise them and their identity with those of our enemies.

"Vanoc" wrote on February 20, 1916, the following words, which should be carefully weighed in all their full meaning:

> Ships with steam up waiting for weeks at a time in the Channel, for want of organisation, have cost the taxpayer thousands of pounds for demurrage. The artificial rise in freight is itself an effective blockade of England. That blockade is the work of the Invisible Hand.
>
> Civilian doctors are overworked, while many doctors in Government service are hard put to it to find work until midday. Of all the events that have happened since the beginning of the War, the refusal of the late Ministry to hold a court-martial on the loss of the "Formidable" is probably the most dramatic and the most effective demonstration of the power of the Invisible Hand. I am not free to tell the true story. When it is told it will be found that the Invisible Hand was hard at work during the Irish troubles and in the Curragh Camp affair before the outbreak of war.
>
> Captain Loxley and his faithful dog friend were drowned from the bridge of a ship handed over to the enemy by the Invisible Hand. The loss of Sir Christopher Craddock's squadron was the work of the Invisible Hand. Influencing honest Britons to organise the destruction of one of their

cruiser squadrons, the deed was easily done. Lord Fisher of Kilverstone has never consciously been under the control of the Invisible Hand, but in his work at the Hague Conference he and Sir Charles Otley, both most honourable and noble-minded English gentlemen, were the unconscious instruments of the Invisible Hand.

The bogey of the neutral Powers is a fiction concocted in the damp, sinister palm of the Invisible Hand. At the meeting at Cannon Street Hotel on February 14, 1916, Lord Devonport made it clear to London men of business that an occult force is at work able to use the resources of the British Empire to feed, arm, succour, and strengthen Germany.

The writer went on to point out that of all the triumphs of the Invisible Hand there was none greater than its successful manipulation of events which led to the escape of the "Goeben" and the "Breslau"; to the war with Turkey; to the death or disablement of 206,000 men of our race in the Gallipoli Peninsula; and in conclusion he wrote:

> The finger-prints of the Invisible Hand show that it has a sense of humour. We have not only been steadily checked or defeated on land for eighteen months, but we have been contemptuously checked or defeated. When the last troops left Gallipoli an aeroplane hovered over the farewell scene. A paper was dropped on which was inscribed, "We don't want to lose you, but we think you ought to go." Between the Scylla of silly optimism and the Charybdis of ignorant pessimism there is a narrow strait. To steer our course we must take the Invisible Hand off the helm. We can win this War, but no longer can we win it easily. That feat is possible only if the Fleet is unshackled and the methods that are so successful at sea are applied to the administration of the land. The appointment of Mr Joseph Pease—a Quaker and a president of the Peace Society—to the Ministry at the present time is a piece of work upon which the Invisible Hand is to be warmly congratulated.

If we are to win the War, the identity of this Invisible Hand must be exposed and its sinister influence defeated. We have seen it at work in a hundred devious ways—the protection of the enemy alien, the amazing leniency shown towards spies, the splendid efforts of one department strangled by the red tape of another, the protection of German-owned property and funds, the provision of delights at Donington Hall and other

Hun hostels; indeed, the whole of the "Don't-hurt-the-poor-German" policy which has been the amazement of ourselves and neutrals alike.

It was this Invisible Hand which destroyed the splendid Dominion Parliament House at Ottawa. Indeed, the Invisible Hand has been responsible for no fewer than fifty-eight incendiary fires in factories engaged in war work in the United States; and by its sinister direction large quantities of our merchant shipping, with passengers and crews, have been sent to its doom. It was the fatal Invisible Hand which blew up the great explosive factory in Havre; the Invisible Hand which suborned the despicable fellow Lincoln, ex-M.P., to become a traitor and endeavour to lead our Grand Fleet into a cunningly-prepared trap laid for it by the "Navy of the Kiel Canal." Therefore one wonders what may be the next blow dealt against us by this mysterious unknown influence, which seems to be the hand of Satan set upon us.

Is it, indeed, the Invisible Hand which to-day refuses to allow some of our Government Departments to be cleansed of the Teuton taint?

Let us take off the gloves and fight this treacherous, unscrupulous, and untrustworthy foe with a firm and heavy fist. We must coddle the Hun no longer. In the past the Home Department has been far too lenient towards the enemy in our midst; and though there are signs of improvement, yet much more remains to be done.

In these days of the Zeppelin menace and daylight raids by Black Cross aeroplanes there is a distinct and ever-present peril in allowing so many enemy aliens to be at large. Further, it is hardly reassuring to Englishmen that, while they are going forward to train and to fight, their places in business and elsewhere may be taken by enemy aliens who have been officially exempted from internment.

The last published official figures given in the House of Commons by the Home Department show that no fewer than 7,233 enemy aliens have been exempted. In the London area alone there were still at large 9,355 male enemy aliens and 8,207 female enemy aliens, while 471 male enemy aliens were still allowed to reside and wander in prohibited areas.

I maintain that if we mean to win — and we do — this state of things must cease. I have raised my voice against it on many occasions. And because I have dared to do so I have received many threats and warnings of an untimely end from these uninterned gentry who are allowed to go and come about London and other large cities, eager and ready to assist the enemy should a raid either by air or land be attempted upon us.

Already we have seen what spies have accomplished in America, and how widespread is all their plots. The recent proceedings in the New York Courts and the official publication of the correspondence found upon the spies Von Papen and Boy-Ed is still fresh in the memory of readers.

Not only in America, in Canada, and in South Africa—where maps were found ready printed showing that colony as a German colony!—but also in Australia, there has lately been revealed the subtle influence of this same Invisible Hand.

The *Melbourne Age*, one of the most responsible journals in Australia, published a long exposure of the whole series of plots in its issues in the first week of January, 1916.

In one, under the heading "Treachery in Excelsis," it said:

> We come now to Germany's supreme act of treachery in our regard. It will be recollected that just prior to the War Australia was visited by the British Association for the Advancement of Science for the purpose of holding here its annual international conference. Our visitors and guests comprised the most eminent men of science from all countries in the world. Germany sent four of her most distinguished professors, viz, Dr Albert Penck, Dr E. Goldstein, Dr Graebner, and Dr Pringsheim. These learned gentlemen still lingered in the Commonwealth when war was declared. They immediately approached the Federal Government for permission to return to Germany, representing that they were international scientists, and therefore neutrals, and that although by accident of birth German citizens, they belonged to the whole world, and ought not to be detained. The Commonwealth Government assented to this proposition, and merely required the savants to take the oath of neutrality. Dr Eugen Goldstein and Dr Albert Penck promptly took the oath. The former went off to Java; the latter took ship to England.

Dr Graebner and Dr Pringsheim appeared to be more dilatory than their *confrères*, and raised all sorts of objections. These, however, were overruled by the Australian authorities, and at length they took the oath.

Proceeding, the *Age* says:

> Suspicion fell on them, and their correspondence was intercepted and examined, luckily for us, before they sailed. Their correspondence proved that they were spies, and

they were immediately arrested and interned. Dr Eugen Goldstein got clear away. But not so Dr Albert Penck. The last-named professor's baggage was overhauled during his journey to Europe under cabled instructions from the war authorities. It contained even more complete information concerning Australia's military preparations and intentions than the correspondence of Graebner and Pringsheim, and it contained in addition most excellent military contour maps of the country surrounding some of our largest capital cities—maps which could have no vestige of use for any purpose than to serve the ends of a German army of invasion. The maps and other information collected by these eminent German scientists were not the work of a day or of a month. They were of a character to prove that Germany had sent the professors to Australia to steal our dearest defence secrets from us, and to repay our hospitality by paving the way for our destruction. The professors, in short, were official German spies. When Dr Penck arrived a prisoner in England he was recognised, moreover, as a German scientist who had in past years led several scientific expeditions to the Isle of Wight, overtly to examine the peculiar geology of the island, but really to spy on Portsmouth, Britain's most important naval base in the English Channel. It is unlikely that Dr Professor Albert Penck will ever see Germany again. When the above facts are considered, what Australian is there can continue to cherish any doubt as to Germany's designs upon the Commonwealth?

From every British colony there has come to us the same story of the clever and ingenious plotting by the enemy alien, just as we have at home daily illustrations of him at his evil work.

Our Allies grappled quickly and drastically with the enemy alien at the very outbreak of war. Russia led the way. Within four days of the declaration of war the Tzar signed a ukase ordering the deportation of all German and Austrian women and children, the internment of all Germans and Austrians, both naturalised and unnaturalised, and, further, the sale of all enemy-owned property by public auction!

Thus a clean and entire sweep was made of the plotters and traitors at one blow, and the German spy system ceased to exist in the Russian Empire.

If we desire to avoid a serious set-back, or even, perhaps, serious disaster when the day of the hammer-blow dawns, we must adopt Russia's example and intern all enemy aliens, both the naturalised and the unnaturalised, irrespective of age or social distinction.

The leopard cannot change his spots, and the born German remains a German to the end of his days. The silly naturalisation farce is far too thin a cloak in these days of our national peril, when we are fighting for our loved ones, our homes, and our honour. I admit that to intern all naturalised Germans would, in many cases, inflict serious discomfort upon many men who have lived with us for years and become to all intents and purposes good Britishers. But in war, and in such a world-war as this, one unfortunately cannot discriminate. Personally I am acquainted with some good naturalised Germans, and I also know some bad and highly suspicious ones.

But surely at this moment, when all factors point to our ultimate victory, we will not allow the Invisible Hand to hold open the gate for the entrance of a barbarous enemy into our land?

The hilarious farce of internment and of exemption a few weeks later must no longer continue. Enemy aliens must no longer be allowed to go on honeymoons, or men go down to conduct their business in the City. Every enemy alien now at large in the United Kingdom must be put again behind stout barbed wire, and Mr McKenna's promise, extracted by that great demonstration of women under Lady Glanusk at the Mansion House, must be kept to the letter to the country.

My demand is that all should be interned, irrespective of whether they have paid their fees and taken the so-called "oath" or not. Every German who becomes naturalised as an Englishman is a traitor to his country, and we have no room for traitors in this country to-day.

If we are to win we must promptly curb the evil activities of these wandering denizens of Lord Haldane's "spiritual home," a sentiment which I express whole-heartedly, and with which I know, from the mass of correspondence daily reaching me, is shared by a very large number of prominent peers, politicians, and citizens.

We must break up the Black Cross of Satan for ever.

Chapter Nine
Compulsory Service Britain's Master-Stroke

No greater evidence could be forthcoming of the absolute determination of the British people to fight the War to a finish than the adoption, in the teeth of our most cherished prejudices, of the principle of compulsory service. Limited in its action though it may be, so watered down, apparently of set purpose, that only a very tiny fraction of men will or need be affected by it, the passing of the Act into law definitely marks a new departure for Britain, and for the first time ranges her alongside the rest of the nations of Europe in emphasising the principle—as old as law itself—that in times of stress and danger the State has the right to call upon all of its sons to come forward and do personal service in defence of the common weal. That, at least, is a very great step in advance. We can be sure it was noted with pleasure and gratification in France and Russia, and with very much the reverse feelings in Germany.

Of all the numerous problems which the War forced suddenly into prominence, this was by far the most urgent and most important. No one imagined, when the War broke out, that in less than eighteen months we should see a measure dealing with compulsory service on the Statute Book of England. That, however, is only to say that few, if any, people realised what the War was going to be; I am firmly convinced that if the problem had been boldly faced in August, 1914, and the people told plainly what it was they were "up against," they would no more have hesitated than they did when the time finally came for a decision. I do not think there is the slightest doubt that, in spite of the occasional clamour of the cranks who, like the poor, are always with us, the Act is on the whole secure in the hearty approval of the great mass of the people.

As those who have done me the honour of reading my books will remember, I have been for many years a convinced advocate of the principle of compulsory national service *for all*. The principle is now adopted in part, and it would serve no good purpose to go again into the arguments for and against it. But there are one or two points to which, even in such a book as this, attention may we usefully drawn. We have to remember that for the first time in our history we have undertaken the responsibility of waging a land war on a national scale. That is to say, we have taken the field with nations whose armies consist literally of the nation in arms.

By hook or by crook we have to maintain our position. Magnificent as has been the response to the call for volunteers, it could not be expected that it would be sufficient under such conditions, partly, of course, because our people were confronted by a set of conditions to which they were absolutely strangers. It was not that there was any real decline in their patriotism—that I do not believe for a moment. Shirkers and slackers, of course, there were and are, as there have always been and will always be in every nation under the sun. But upon the whole the response of the manhood of England to the appeal for recruits was so magnificent that we are justified in regarding it with every feeling of pride. And, convinced as I am of the benefits which national service confers upon the nations which adopt it, I should have been glad from the bottom of my heart if we had been able to carry this War to a successful conclusion on the principles of voluntarism which has served us so long. It would have been a glorious vindication of those very principles of liberty which this country went into the War to uphold.

But, after all, there is no derogation from the liberty of the subject in being called upon to serve the State which protects him and to which he owes the very possibility of existence in peace and comfort. That principle is as old as liberty itself; without it liberty, as we understand it to-day, would never have been won; perhaps civilisation itself would have been centuries farther back. It is an utter misrepresentation to speak as though the conscript, which has been made a word of evil omen by the very journals which a few short years ago were holding up everything German for our admiration, were a much-to-be-pitied individual with no rights and no liberties. Because German drill-sergeants happen to be brutes—as the Germans *en masse* have proved themselves to be—there is no reason for thinking that we need share their brutality. The experience of France, of Switzerland, of Italy—indeed, of every country except Germany that has adopted the principle of compulsion—does not support the comfortable and lazy theory that brutes are created by the "militarism" which some of our facile writers fail entirely to understand. It is the innate brutality of the Prussian which has produced the horrible results we see springing from German militarism, not the principle of compulsion introduced as a matter of national self-preservation.

We are an insular Power, and as such we have been able in the past to rely almost entirely upon our Fleet for protection against our enemies; our land campaigns of the past, glorious though they have often been, bear little relation to the present struggle, in which the greatest battles of bygone days—battles which have decided the fate of nations—would be dwarfed to mere incidents hardly worth a paragraph in the official report. The campaigns of to-day are being fought not by armies but by nations in arms—a very important distinction. Only a few short years ago, when armies were tiny compared with the vast hosts of to-day, a single battle often decided a war. To-day battles which dwarf the greatest struggles of the past into comparative insignificance are nothing more than mere incidents in the far-flung lines of the contending hosts. And the huge size of modern armies has been made possible only by the system which takes the young and able-bodied and compulsorily trains them with a view to military service when war comes. We did not invent that system; indeed, we refused to adopt it long after it had come into operation among all other European nations. But we have to meet the system in operation in the field against us, and we have hitherto been trying with hastily improvised armies to beat nations which have spent half a century in training their manhood in the use of arms. I rejoice that such marvellous efforts have been made, and that such wonderful results have been achieved under the voluntary system. But that system can never produce "the nation in arms," and it is emphatically "the nation in arms" that is required if we are to beat the Germans. Before this frightful struggle ends we shall certainly require to make every effort of which we, as a nation and an Empire, are capable.

It is a little difficult to understand the opposition to the principle of compulsory service. By the common law of almost all nations the State has the right to call upon the individual for assistance in protecting the State against the common enemy. I do not see, indeed, how this right can be disputed, for to dispute it would be to cut at the very foundations of organised society. One can, of course, readily understand wide differences of opinion as to the advisability or necessity of adopting a compulsory system, especially in the middle of a great war, but against the principle itself I fail to see any valid argument. *Salus populi lex suprema*. If the interests of the nation demand the introduction of compulsion, whether during a war or not, I cannot understand how it can be opposed either in principle or as a matter of expediency.

Now it must be quite clearly understood that, so far as Britain is concerned, the adoption of the principle of compulsion was purely a matter of expediency, and those lifelong opponents of compulsory service who found themselves able to support the Act sacrificed none of their convictions or principles in doing so. We had reached a stage in the War when the problem of finding enough men to keep our armies in the field up to full strength had become critical. Mr Asquith had pledged himself—quite rightly, as I think—that the married men who enlisted under the Derby group system should not be called up while any considerable number of single slackers remained deaf to every call that was made upon them. In this I believe he was absolutely right, and I believe he had behind him the vast preponderance of intelligent opinion in the country, including, though the fact has been disputed, the bulk of the working-class population. We were unquestionably drafting into the Army too large a proportion of married men, and widows and orphans were being made at a rate that was positively appalling. It was quite obvious that something must be done to put a stop to this condition of things, and the famous pledge of Mr Asquith was the result. And when it was found that the unmarried men still remained outside the Army, the passage into law of a measure of compulsion could be nothing more than a matter of time.

The Act was frankly a temporising measure, and my own personal belief is that it does not go nearly far enough. Mr Asquith has declared that he does not think the situation calls for a measure of general compulsion, and he must be in possession of facts which are hidden from the public. Present indications suggest that he is right; whether he was wise to bolt and bar the door to general compulsion so emphatically as he did is another matter. It was certainly a very remarkable statement of Lord Kitchener, reported to the House of Commons by Mr Walter Long, that the Act as it stood would provide all the men required to ensure victory, a statement which seems hardly to have attracted the attention that it deserved. Both Mr Asquith and Lord Kitchener may be right, and it is certainly true that our prospects are brighter than they have been for many months.

In view of what may conceivably happen in the future, there is one misconception with regard to national service which it is perhaps worth while to try to clear up. It is too hastily assumed that the men who are swept into the net of a compulsory system are necessarily drafted to the fighting ranks. This, of course, is a mistake pure and simple. One of the greatest advantages of the compulsory system is that by its means men can be employed just at the work where their services are most needed. It is quite certain that had we had a compulsory service system in operation when the War broke out we should have seen less of the enlistment into the fighting services of men whose brains and muscles were urgently needed in other directions. We should not, for instance, have seen three hundred thousand miners sent to the trenches while we were short of coal at home; we should not have seen our munition works held up through shortage of skilled labour consequent upon high-class mechanics joining the fighting line. Each man would have been sent to serve where he was most needed, and this, it seems to me, is one of the strongest arguments that can be adduced in favour of the principle of compulsion.

Under all the circumstances the adoption of compulsion has been achieved with wonderfully little disturbance. There have been none of those wild outbreaks of popular passion which were so strenuously forecasted by the thick-and-thin opponents of compulsion. As my readers are, of course, aware, the adoption of compulsion by President Lincoln during the American Civil War was followed by serious disturbances which had to be suppressed by troops brought from the front, and which caused grievous loss of life. We have seen nothing of the kind here, and I do not think we are likely to do so. The country is united and determined to win the War, and the anti-conscription efforts of certain misguided folk have been received with the contempt they deserved. The quiet acceptance of the Act is all the more remarkable when we remember that owing to the operation of the censorship the people generally were very ill-informed about the War, and it is certain that up to quite a recent date they did not realise all that was involved or the magnitude of the task we had undertaken. The wonder is not that a system of compulsion became necessary, but that under the bad system of secrecy we succeeded in raising armies totalling some three millions of men by the voluntary plan. There could be no greater testimony to the genuine patriotism of the workers of England. Happily, the country is now more fully awake to the facts of the situation, and has achieved a better realisation of what the struggle really means.

Nothing has been more remarkable than the attitude of Labour on this subject. We have been told over and over again that the workers of Britain would never accept the principle of compulsion; we have found, in fact, that it has gained the support of all that is best in the Labour ranks. There can be no doubt that one of the greatest difficulties in the way was the hasty and ill-advised resolution passed by the Trade Union Congress at Bristol in January, 1915. It is not necessary to enter into the causes which led to the passing of that most unhappy resolution. Suffice it to say that it put the Trade Unionists in the position of declaring that they would prefer to see the Empire go to ruin rather than see the principle of compulsion introduced. I felt at the time—and subsequent events have justified my belief—that this was a grave libel upon the patriotism of our workers. The Merthyr by-election, when the official Liberal and Labour candidate was decisively beaten by an Independent candidate, who won a tremendous victory on a straight compulsion issue in a constituency which had always been regarded as a stronghold of every idea that would be opposed to compulsion, came as a dramatic surprise. In all probability that election did more than any other single thing to make compulsion possible, and it certainly showed that the working classes of this country had changed their minds on a subject on which it was supposed their minds were irrevocably made up.

We were to learn later that their opposition to compulsion was based not on compulsion itself, but on the fear that conscripts would be used to settle industrial troubles as was done in the case of the French railway strike. But the assurance on this head given by Mr Asquith seems to have removed what latent hostility there was to the proposals of the Government, and as a result there is every prospect that the Act will work as smoothly as we could desire or expect.

Under all the circumstances it is easy to sympathise with the attitude of the Labour leaders when they met for the Trade Union Congress of 1916. They found themselves faced with the resolution passed twelve months before under very different circumstances. They knew better—they had been told frankly by Lord Kitchener—the extreme urgency of our needs, and they certainly had no desire to embarrass the Government or stand in the way of the Empire winning the victory. But we have to recognise the facts of human nature. It is not easy for any of us to eat our words, and yet it seemed as if the Congress must either do so or take up a frankly disloyal attitude. They were deeply pledged against compulsion, and it needs no very powerful effort of the imagination to see that they were in a position of some difficulty.

Luckily, a way was found out of the seeming *impasse*. The Congress decided to adhere to its resolution condemning compulsory service as a matter of principle, but it decisively defeated a proposal to work for the repeal of the Act which had already been passed. The national spirit of compromise came strongly to the front. I wrote before the Congress met: "However difficult it may be for them to swallow the very definite declaration of the last Congress, I think the majority of them, if the present recruiting movement fails, will loyally accept the logical sequel." Those words were abundantly justified. In view of the partial failure of Lord Derby's scheme, the Congress took the natural and proper view. Abating none of their strongly held objections to compulsion, they accepted the Bill as the lesser of two evils: better put up with a modified measure of compulsion now than endure defeat, with all the horrors that it would imply, in the future. And there can be no reasonable doubt that that view is far more widely held among the working classes than is shown by the voting of a caucus in which the most extreme Socialist and Syndicalist element has secured a measure of representation which it does not deserve.

As to whether the Act will give us all the men we need, we can only go on and hope for the best. Lord Kitchener apparently thinks it will, and he ought to be in a position to know. But we have to remember that in modern warfare the drain upon an army and the wastage of men—not only from actual casualties in fighting, but from sickness and other causes—is appalling. It has been officially stated that our losses by wastage from all causes amount to *fifteen per cent, per month* of all the forces in the field. That is to say, that if we have a million men under arms they will have to be replaced every six months! And even this appalling rate of loss might well be exceeded if fighting became very severe; if, for instance, we had to fight battles such as the first and second battles of Ypres. Fighting on an even larger scale, it must be remembered, is only too probable if the Allies undertake the "big push" which shall throw the Huns out of their entrenchments in the West, to say nothing of a possible advance from Salonica and more fighting in Mesopotamia. It will thus be seen that the requirements of the Army in the matter of drafts during the next few months will be on a gigantic scale, and we cannot afford to run the risk of being short of men.

The time is assuredly coming when the German reserves will begin to give out in view of the enormous extent of front they had to defend. That will be the opportunity of the Allies; and unless we are then in a position swiftly to make good all possible losses and fling more and ever more men into the fight to administer the *coup de grâce*, the War may well drag on—almost certainly it would drag on—to an inconclusive ending which would be only one remove less disastrous than defeat. It is against such a possibility as this that we have to guard, and we can only do so by deciding that, cost what it may—whether by compulsion or not, whether only the single men are taken or whether every able-bodied man shall be swept into the ranks—the fighting lines of our armies shall be maintained at fighting strength. So much we owe to ourselves, to our Empire, and to the thousands of gallant souls who have given their all in order that we may live out our lives in peace. To falter now would be not only ingratitude to the fallen, but would be the blackest treachery to everything which we know as civilisation.

Mr Asquith has declared that he will be no party to any further measure of general compulsion. I can only assume that he means by this that he is confident of victory under existing circumstances, and I hope and believe he is right. But it would be foolish to disguise from ourselves that war is a very "chancy" and uncertain business, and that there are few subjects upon which it is more foolhardy to dogmatise. We have seen something during this War of the wreck which has fallen on the reputations of the military "experts." And, believe we never so strongly in victory, there is no disguising the fact that our expectations may be falsified by events. In such a case—supposing we require more men than we can obtain by the measure of limited compulsion that we have adopted—are we to lose the War for want of stronger measures? That will hardly, I think, be contended, and if the men wanted are not forthcoming they must be found by sterner measures.

"We must win or go under" is the great truth we have to keep for ever before our eyes and before the eyes of our fellow-countrymen. And to secure victory there must be no half-measures. If Mr Asquith finds himself unable to undertake the task of raising the men urgently needed—should more be required—other men and other measures must fill the gaps. On that point, at least, there must be no faltering.

I do not believe the workers to-day are troubling themselves very greatly about the nice ethical points for or against the principle of compulsion. They are judging on broad lines, and I am confident they view the question in a light very different from that in which they regarded it when the War broke out. Since those days they have learnt from the example of Belgium and France what is involved in German rule, and their change of views has been helped by a realisation of the magnitude of the task which lies before us. They know that the War is for us a matter of self-preservation, and I believe such opposition to compulsion as still survives comes solely from other and more doctrinaire classes. What the country asks from the Government is a clear and unmistakable lead. If the Government will but take the nation fully and frankly into its confidence, if those who are entitled to speak for the nation will call upon the nation for the greatest and supremest effort of its history, I do not believe there will be any hesitation in the response whether we decide to extend the principle of compulsion or not. I believe the result will be to astonish and confound those who have more or less openly suggested that the spirit of England is not what it was, and that the Englishman has lost in a great measure the stern invincibility and determination which in his forefathers made England what she is and has always been.

So far we have adopted what Lord Lansdowne has described as "a homeopathic dose" of compulsion. The description is apt; I hope the dose will be sufficient to dispel the disease. But there is one point on which we must be on our guard: the list of "reserved" trades whose men are not to be taken for the Army is growing at an alarming rate. We know that one of the results of this has been to cut down very seriously the number of men who ought to have joined the colours under Lord Derby's group scheme; we must be careful lest we lose more men than we should from the same cause under the Compulsion Act. It is necessary, of course, that our trade must be kept going as far as possible; otherwise we shall not be able to pay for the War.

But we must remember at the same time that victory is and must be our first consideration, for without this we shall have no trade to look after. And if, in our eagerness to conserve our trade, we neglect or starve the fighting forces, we shall pay a terrible and appalling penalty. That is the worst of doing things by halves; one generally finds in the long run that it would have been better and cheaper to have made a good job at the first. It is more than likely that the "reserved" occupations will turn out to be the crux of the whole question, and the rapidly growing lists give rise to a feeling of apprehension as to whether we shall not fail, if they are extended indefinitely, to get the men we require. I earnestly hope that this most important subject is receiving careful attention, and that we shall have such periodical revisions of the lists as experience may show to be necessary. All will be well so long as we do not risk, for the sake of supposed trade advantages, any shortage of men in the actual fighting lines.

The willing adoption by our people of the principle of compulsion has been Britain's master-stroke in this war. Nothing else, I am convinced, could have had such an effect upon our friends, our enemies, and the neutral nations, whether friendly to us or the reverse. Nothing else could have shown so clearly the unalterable determination of the British people, or proved so unmistakably that at length—late, it is true, but better late than never—the cold and deadly pertinacity of Britain, the dour temper which never knows when it is beaten and never lets go, has been fully roused. Britain, it is said, wins but one victory in every war, but that victory is the last. That is one victory we mean to win in this War, if it takes us ten or twenty years to do it. We fought Napoleon for twenty years; we won the last victory at Waterloo. It will not be twenty years before the Allies win the victory that shall put an end to the pretensions of the upstart who aspires to be the Napoleon of the twentieth century.

Chapter Ten
Germany's Colossal Blunders

It is the fashion of our arm-chair critics and pessimists to talk and write as though all the triumphs of the campaign belonged to Germany, while all the mistakes and misfortunes were the exclusive attributes of the Allies. The perfection of the German military machine is held up eternally for our admiration; we are told day by day—and several times a day—to pay tributes of wondering admiration to the marvels Germany has accomplished. It is pointed out to us how much of her enemies' territory she has occupied, and even, sometimes, how impossible it will ever be to turn her out. We are even besought by certain faint-hearts to make peace while we can on the "generous" terms which Germany has announced herself willing to concede if we will only admit her over-lordship of Europe, an admission we have not the slightest intention of making either now or in the future.

Now I am not going to deny that we and the rest of the Allies have made mistakes, alike in policy, strategy, and tactics; in fact, if you will, in every field of the War. But the nation that can wage war without making mistakes has yet to be discovered, and it is certain that if such a nation ever arises it will speedily dominate the world. Let it be admitted that we have made mistakes in plenty, and that we shall make many more before we see the end of this terrible business. It still remains true that the mistakes of the Allies have been as dust in the balance compared with those made by Germany. I fear many of my readers may think this a hard saying, but I shall try to demonstrate its literal truth.

The first and greatest of the mistakes made by the Allied nations was that they failed to foresee years ago that the War was inevitable, and that Germany was firmly resolved that it should break out just when it was most convenient to her. There we have, in a nutshell, the basis of all our troubles. Of Germany's intentions in the matter there has not been a shadow of doubt; thinkers like Mr Frederic Harrison, and soldiers like Lord Roberts, saw very clearly what was coming, and even that much-abused individual, "the man in the street," has for years had more than an uneasy suspicion that Germany was plotting mischief. The famous Kruger telegram, the trouble at Samoa, the visit of the "Panther" to Agadir, the numberless occasions during the past few years when Germany has interfered in matters which were no concern of hers, ought surely to have been enough to put us on our guard. And on top of all this we have Lord Haldane's bland admission that he came back from his Berlin visit feeling "very uneasy" as to Germany's intentions. Just after war broke out a very old friend of my own—a man who knows Germany and the Germans well—wrote to remind me that seven or eight years ago he prophesied that war would break out in 1914, when the Kiel Canal widening was to be completed.

I do not see how, in the face of all these facts, we can pretend for an instant that we had not ample warning of the cataclysm which has overtaken the world. I do not say that we were any blinder than the rest of those who are now on our side, but I do say that our failure to make ready in time was the most powerful factor in bringing about the War, and gave Germany an initial advantage which we are now only beginning to wrest from her. For Germany was ready—ready down to the last proverbial button on her soldiers' gaiters—and nothing but the gigantic blunders she has made in the conduct of the War has saved civilisation from being overrun by the hordes whom the Kaiser is proud to recognise as the modern successors of Attila. Had the nations of Europe dropped their mutual jealousies five years ago, and clearly warned Germany that the first act of aggression on her part would bring all of them into the field against her, how different would have been the course of modern history!

Let us go back to the beginning of things and examine some of Germany's blunders from the very outset. We have, in the first place, ample evidence that Germany counted with confidence that the War would be short—that she would, in effect, repeat her triumph of 1870-71 on a grander scale. We know that this was so from the evidence of her own writers and statesmen and people, both before and since the War began. The programme was, on paper, delightfully simple. In view of the solemn treaties into which Germany had entered, France had refrained from fortifying her Belgian frontier.

This simplified matters for Germany. Belgian neutrality was to be contemptuously violated and France attacked on her weakest front, the inconvenient line of fortresses along the Rhine being thus carefully avoided. Belgium, it was calculated, would not dare to resist her mighty adversary, or, if she did, so much the worse for her. France was to be shattered in a brief campaign—so effectively shattered, as Germans themselves boasted, that she could never again be a menace. England, fat and lazy England, it was confidently reckoned, would not interfere, or could not interfere in time on land. France disabled permanently, the victorious Germans were to turn on slow-moving Russia, whose mobilisation could not be completed for months, and who was to be hopelessly smashed by the weight of the combined Austro-German arms before she could get her giant legions into the field. Serbia, of course, the ostensible cause of all the trouble, would be of no account, and could be crushed with hardly an effort, leaving the way open for German domination through Bulgaria and Turkey, and on to Persian Mesopotamia and the East. England, the chief adversary in the German dream of world-power, was to be left to be settled with at a more auspicious season.

Now, we have had our trials and disappointments since war broke out, and we shall have more, but I ask in sober seriousness if a fraction of our plans have gone wrong so completely as has every single factor upon which Germany counted for the success of her scheme? We know what happened. Belgium refused to barter her honour for peace, and it is beyond question that the three weeks' delay her heroic resistance secured for the Allies saved Europe. France showed herself as great as of old, and her sons flung themselves into the fight with a gallantry which has proved unconquerable. The outrage on Belgium brought England into the fray, and her "contemptible little army" played no inglorious part in shattering the German advance. Russia mobilised with a speed which startled the world, and her legions were thundering at the gates of Germany weeks ahead of what the Germans had been pleased to regard as the "schedule time." Serbia threw back the Austrian armies in an appalling defeat, and in a very few weeks Germany must have realised that she had to face that long and dragging war which every single one of her military writers had foretold must prove ruinous to her. When I say "Germany" I mean, of course, the German military authorities; the German people were kept in an abysmal ignorance of the facts of the case. It is not too much to say that within three months of the outbreak of the War the German Higher Command must have begun to realise that whatever might be the outcome of the struggle it was not going to be a German triumph. And we may be sure that they have since realised it with ever-growing clearness.

It cannot, of course, be supposed that the Germans neglected altogether the possibility that England might join the Alliance against them, though there is very good ground for the belief that they were vastly surprised that we should fight them over "a scrap of paper." But they took the risk, and they took it the more readily because they had for years been assured that England, if not too proud to fight, was at least too wealthy and too lazy to have any stomach for such an enterprise as an armed conflict with the supermen of Germany. Hence the insolent offers that were made to buy us off at the expense of France. And there is little doubt that the Germans believed that even if we did come in we should be of trifling account in the land war, while they reckoned that they could at least keep their Fleet in safety until their submarines had either starved us into submission or had so weakened our Fleet that it could hope to operate at sea with a reasonable chance of success. They thought, in fact, that as a factor in a continental war England could safely be neglected. Certain is it that they never for a moment dreamed that England could raise and put into the field armies on the scale of millions which, in respect of equipment and training, would rival or eclipse anything that Germany could show to the world.

Yet that is precisely what England has done. Man for man the British Army is superior to that of Germany, and it is better trained and better equipped. And it has not yet developed its full fighting force, while the armies of Germany, weakened by eighteen months of terrific fighting, have long passed their zenith. Germany has squandered her best troops, and is beginning at last to fall back on inferior organisations; we have millions of the pick of the nation who have not yet taken the field. They will do so in good time, and with ample reserves behind them. "General French's contemptible little army" has been a surprise for the Kaiser.

So much for German blunders on land; what can we say about her blunders at sea? The policy of attrition has failed lamentably, and we are not yet starved out by the submarines or greatly perturbed by the threats of new "frightfulness" which periodically emanate from Berlin. Our Fleet is actually stronger than it was when war began; Germany has lost far more in proportion, and her losses in cruisers—the eyes and ears of the battle squadrons—have been particularly disastrous. The German flag, except as shown by the submarine pirates and occasional raiders, has vanished from the oceans of the world, and with it has gone Germany's gigantic overseas trade, which was the very life-blood of her industrial prosperity.

The probable attitude of England towards the War must have been the subject of a good deal of speculation in the Wilhelmstrasse before Germany threw down the gauntlet to the world, and here again we have an excellent example of the blundering of German diplomacy. We shall never know exactly what advice Prince Lichnowsky gave from London to his Imperial master. It is said that he warned the Kaiser not to allow himself to run away with the idea that England was too much occupied with internal disputes to fight. However that may be, there is every reason for thinking that those who at the time were preaching the possibility of civil war in Ireland did much to convince Germany that the time was ripe for the great adventure. The Germans failed, in the blundering German way, to realise that while England's troubles are her own, her cause is the cause of humanity and civilisation, and that the first threat of attack on either would bring her warring parties into one formidable cohesion which would defy any possible menace of trouble within. That is precisely what happened, and it must have been the surprise of their lives for the German diplomats.

The Colonies, as we know, represented in the eyes of the Germans so much ripe fruit ready at a touch to drop from the rotten parent tree. India was seething with revolt—according to the German war party; South Africa was represented as ready to throw itself into the lap of Germany for the sake of shaking off the very shadowy British yoke. Can any of the mistakes we have made in politics or strategy match this record of blundering ineptitude? We know how India and the Dominions and South Africa responded to the call of Empire. India, Canada, and Australia have sealed anew with their blood the tie which binds them to the Mother Country; to-day a Dutch South African is busy turning the Germans out of the last bit which remains to them of their once huge Colonial Empire. Perhaps we blundered in our diplomacy in the Balkans, but at least we have not blundered, as the Germans have done, in every part of the world where chance of blundering lay open to us.

So far I have dealt only with German blunders, political and military, in anticipation of war. Let us turn now to some of her blunders in the actual conduct of operations in the field. I do not mean the blunders of subordinates, but the mistakes of strategy and policy which are capable of ruining the best-planned and most carefully-thought-out campaign.

The violation of the neutrality of Belgium may have been an advantage from the point of view of strategy; whether it was or not, the Germans thought it was, and that was good enough for them. If it would be an advantage to Germany, they were prepared to undertake it, and treaty obligations troubled them not one whit. That it would instantly range all civilised opinion against them seems never to have entered their heads. But even after they had crossed Belgium their grand strategy was lamentable. They succumbed to the lure of Paris at a time when they ought to have been thinking solely of the northern ports of France, which were practically open to them, and Paris proved to be the magnet which drew them on to their undoing.

The menace to Paris roused the French to fury, and produced superhuman exertions which a contest on the soil of France elsewhere might very possibly not have evoked. Moreover, the German threat at Paris gave the English time to come into action with what proved to be decisive effect. Was there no German blundering here? What, I wonder, would have been the result if the Germans had in those early days of the War flung all their force at the coasts of Northern France? How should we have met the menace with the sea bases largely in German hands? What would have been our position in the naval warfare to-day?

And even with Paris almost in their grasp, the Germans failed—failed as lamentably as they possibly could. They never even suspected the existence of that great army of Paris which General Manoury had formed under their very noses, as it were. And when on that fatal day Von Kluck found himself faced with a new danger from that great army which issued from the gates of the French capital, what did he do? He committed a blunder which has been condemned by every military writer by trying to march his retreating columns across the front of the British Army which lay parallel to the line of his retreat. No doubt he reckoned that after its terrific gruelling in the great retreat the British Army was in no shape to take offensive action against him. But it was his business to know, not to think; probably his Teutonic arrogance led him to believe that no troops after such a retreat could stand up against the pick of the German arms. He was soon undeceived. General Joffre struck at once and with all his might, seizing with the truest military genius and insight the psychological moment. The French and British flung themselves upon the badly shaken enemy, and in a few short days the victory of the Marne had been won.

Whatever we may think of what has happened since, it is certain that the battle of the Marne will be recognised in the future as one of the great decisive battles of the world. For it smashed beyond repair the German strategic scheme. German blundering alone made victory possible, for at the time the battle was fought the Germans were unquestionably superior to the Allies in every factor which should have given them the victory had they acted on sound lines. The machine was there—the machine upon which the Germans have all along relied—but the human control broke down, and disaster followed. Among all the mistakes which had been made by the Allies, can the keenest critic discover anything to compare with this?

A prominent feature of the German strategy has been the attack of their infantry in dense masses; their commanders have flung men forward in solid columns in the hope of overwhelming their enemies by sheer weight of numbers. This has been a matter of considered policy; attack in this formation has been practised at the German manoeuvres for years. The German commanders took no notice of those military critics of other nations who assured them that with modern weapons such tactics could only meet with irretrievable disaster. With true Prussian cocksureness, and knowing nothing of war since the days when quick-firing guns and magazine rifles had revolutionised war, they insisted that they were right, and that German hardihood would be proof against even the most appalling losses. They have practised what they preached, since there was no possibility of re-training their men in time of war, and the result has been daughter on such a scale as the world has never seen. Not once, but a hundred times have German massed attacks across open country simply melted away before the fire which greeted them, and in this way Germany has lost untold thousands of men who, had they been intelligently used, might have gone far to win the War.

This, again, is not an example of the mistakes made by subordinate commanders in the field, but a settled matter of policy approved by the highest German military experts, and proved hopelessly wrong under the actual test of war. Attacks by massed guns and not by massed infantry have been the most powerful factors in winning the German successes. We saw in the appalling slaughter of the great battle of Ypres how little infantry, resolute and well handled, have to fear from the advance of men who simply come on in solid masses to be shot down.

It has long been a part of the German creed that "frightfulness" in war pays. The avowed German policy is that a conquered nation shall be left "nothing but its eyes to weep with." The idea, of course, is that any nation which has the misfortune to incur Germany's resentment shall be so completely terrorised and oppressed that anything in the shape of a spirit of resistance shall be utterly crushed out in a welter of blood and savagery before which a civilised community must sink appalled. Here we have a simple explanation of the crimes which staggered the world after the invasion of Belgium. It was all a part of the German policy that the Belgian civilians should be tortured, outraged, and murdered, that their towns should be laid waste, that monuments of an ancient civilisation which even the Huns of old respected should be destroyed by the newest apostles of "kultur." Eight hundred civilians were massacred at Dinant in cold blood to show the Belgians how hopeless it was to resist Germany; hundreds of women have been violated in the same cause; hundreds of churches have been destroyed; dozens of villages have been laid in ashes. And all this, let it be remembered—let it, indeed, never be forgotten—was the result not of war-maddened soldiers losing their heads and their manhood, but of a deliberate policy deliberately adopted by the rulers of Germany.

In every war and in every army there happen, in hot blood, incidents over which humanity weeps; human nature being what it is, excesses are sometimes unavoidable. But it has been left to modern Germany to elevate murder and violence and destruction to a science; she has in this respect set up a record which would shame a Red Indian, and from which the great warring and plundering nations of old would have shrunk appalled. The history of war for centuries has given us nothing to approach in horror the German devastation of Belgium and of Poland, unless we except the massacres of the Armenians by Germany's Turkish Allies with Germany's connivance and approval.

Now I am quite certain that the criminality of these proceedings troubles the German nation not one whit. But I am equally certain that they will be seriously troubled when they realise that "frightfulness" is what is in their eyes far worse than a crime; it is a blunder. When the German Hyde has recovered from his debauch of bestiality and violence, we may expect the German Jekyll to begin assuring us that he is really a very decent sort of fellow after all. For Jekyll will come some day to realise that Hyde's crimes have not helped his cause, that Hyde was really not merely a savage—that he could accept without a pang—but that he was a sad blunderer. That, to the German, is the real unforgivable sin. And blunderer in his campaign of "frightfulness" the German assuredly has been and is. The policy of terrorism has been a complete failure; it has failed in Belgium, it has failed in France, it has failed in Serbia, it has failed in Poland, it has failed afloat, and it has failed in the air. It is a record of blood and murder unredeemed by a solitary success; it has steeled the hearts and the resolution of all to whom it has been applied, and among the neutral nations it has provoked feelings which cause nausea whenever Germany is mentioned.

In the face of unmentionable horrors—unmentionable except in the pages of official reports—Belgium has steadily refused to have any traffic whatever with the Huns; her soldiers are preparing to-day to take their full meed of vengeance of those who have made a desert of her smiling land. Serbia is still unconquered, though her land is occupied and devastated. Poland spurns the German yoke. Britain not only is undismayed, but is more firmly resolved than ever to make an end for good and all of German pretensions. Russia is striking shrewd blows, and will strike yet harder in the near future. Italy is steadily preparing for greater things. France is her own great self, and is waiting with unconquerable resolution for the appointed hour. Only in Germany and her Allies do we discover a growing spirit of apprehension and of weakening purpose. Can we say in the face of all these things that the policy of "frightfulness" has been anything but a blunder of the first magnitude?

It is commonly assumed that German savagery reached its height in the sinking of the "Lusitania," and certainly that crime struck the conscience of civilisation more forcibly than the horrors in Belgium, partly because it was a direct object-lesson of the depths to which modern Germany was capable of descending. But in sober truth the "Lusitania" outrage was nothing in comparison with what had been done in Belgium. There Germany's record of horrors was so atrocious that no respectable newspaper could reproduce the evidence gathered by the French Official Commission, and only those who had read the original could form any conception of what the reality must have been. The victims of the "Lusitania" at least died swiftly and comparatively painlessly; Belgium's lot was in too many cases such that death would have been infinitely preferable. But to the sinking of the "Lusitania" is to be attributed the uprising of the wrath of the United States, who saw over a hundred of her citizens simply murdered in cold blood.

It is not for us to criticise the action the United States may think fit to adopt in defence of its own people, but it is certain that nine Americans out of ten are far ahead of their Government in their opinion of what ought to be done. What will be done is a matter for the Americans themselves, and we have no right to interfere. But it is at least to be regretted, in the interest of international morality and good faith, that the United States, as the foremost of the neutral nations, did not see fit to protest against German violation of international law until the interests of American citizens were directly attacked. The failure of the neutral nations to make such a protest has probably done untold harm to the prospects of international agreements in the future. What value, for instance, will the world, in days to come, attach to the proceedings of a Hague Convention whose solemn agreements Germany has been permitted to infringe without a word of protest from neutrals who shared in its deliberations and acquiesced in its decisions?

German disregard of the decencies of international life and her lack of understanding of the feelings of other nations have been abundantly shown in the conspiracy of intimidation which has been carried on in the United States. It seemed quite natural to the Germans that their Embassy in Washington should be made the head centre for plots which were calculated, and intended, to provoke a conflict between the United States and Great Britain. They seem to have been quite incapable of realising that the United States might possibly object to being made the cat's-paw of German diplomacy, just as they seem to have thought that the blowing up of American munition works to prevent supplies reaching the Allies was a proceeding about which Americans could have no real reason to complain. In the same manner they appear to have thought that the forgery of United States passports for the use of their spies in England was a mere trifle, undeserving of the slightest censure, regardless of the fact that no other nation in the world would stoop to such unspeakable meanness.

The result of their blundering is that they have brought themselves within measurable distance of having a war with America on their hands, and but for the patience of President Wilson war would have broken out long ago. It is believed, of course, that for some reasons war with the United States would serve the German purpose at the present moment by giving them an excuse for making peace on the plausible ground that they could not fight the whole world; but whatever may be the truth about this now, it was certainly not the truth in the early days of the War when the Germans were overwhelmingly confident that they could win. Even then they were flouting the United States in every possible way, and showing the greatest contempt for the greatest of the neutral nations. It was all of a piece with the blundering diplomacy which has been exhibited in every quarter of the world.

The complete failure of Germany to placate Italy is another blunder which will have a great effect in the final outcome of the War. Perhaps Austria in those days was not quite so servile to her German masters as she is to-day. In any case the attempt failed; and if we are to measure blunders in diplomacy, we can quite justifiably set the German failure in this respect against our own supposed failure in the Balkans with the confidence that the Germans have at least lost as much as we did—probably they have lost a great deal more. The Germans undoubtedly relied upon Bulgaria to overcome the Serbian resistance, just as they relied upon the Turk to help them turn us out of Egypt and open up a direct German route to Persia and India and the East generally. But what are the facts of the situation? There is every reason to believe that relations between the Germans and their Allies are none too cordial. Bulgar and Turk alike hate Teutonic arrogance, and both are beginning to realise that they have been duped. There is every reason to think that the Bulgars are already repenting of their bargain, while the Turks, in the loss of Erzerum, see a vital blow struck by the Russians at the very heart of their Empire. Moreover, we know that the huge supplies which the Germans hoped to draw from both Turkey and Bulgaria are not forthcoming for the simple reason that they do not exist. Turkey unmistakably is tottering to her final fall, and then, we may well ask, what becomes of the grandiose German plans for an advance on Egypt, Mesopotamia, and India? Can we say that in this direction, more than in others, the German plans have gone well?

The Dardanelles expedition is popularly held to be the greatest blunder of our campaign. But are we quite so sure that, failure though it was, it was all lost effort, or even, as things were, that it was not worth the price we paid? That is a question which will be settled only by the historian of the future. But to those who see in it only the failure of a great effort and the sacrifice of many gallant lives it may be pointed out that it had very important results.

In the first place, it held up at least half a million Turks who would have been very useful elsewhere, it brought the enemy a loss of probably 200,000 men, it sensibly weakened his powers of resistance, and in all probability it very materially assisted the Russians to win their great victory at Erzerum.

It undoubtedly did much to stave off the threatened attack on Egypt and the Suez Canal, and it probably saved our expedition in Mesopotamia from utter disaster. I do not say all these things could not have been achieved otherwise, but I do feel that in balancing gains and losses we have a right to claim that even in the tragedy of the Dardanelles there are compensations to be found if we try to look at the matter in a cool and impartial light. Most unfortunately the issue has been clouded by the introduction of the personal element as between Mr Churchill and Sir John Fisher, and until the heat of that controversy has cooled down it is unlikely that the problem of the Dardanelles will receive anything like fair and adequate consideration.

The worst of our blunders was our unpreparedness, and for it we are paying a heavy price. But since we set our hands to the plough we have made such efforts as no nation has ever made in the history of the world; and if we had made no mistakes in the raising and training and using of three millions of men in warfare of a type of which we have had no previous experience, we should indeed have been the supermen which the Germans proudly believe and boast themselves to be. Our mistakes have been many and grievous; they will be many and grievous in the days that are to come. But at least we are justified in saying that we are not the only blunderers. Germany started the War with the inestimable advantage of complete readiness for the fray; and if she had not made mistakes at least equal to those of the Allies, she would long ago have been mistress of Europe and well on the way to the dominating position in the world of which she dreamed, but which she will never occupy.

Chapter Eleven
Victory with Honour

We shall not sheathe the sword, which we have not lightly drawn, until Belgium recovers in full measure all and more than all that she has sacrificed, until France is secured from the menace of aggression, until the rights of the smaller nationalities of Europe are placed upon an unassailable foundation, until the military domination of Prussia is fully and finally destroyed. That is a great task worthy of a great nation.

Such were the magnificent phrases in which Mr Asquith, at the Guildhall on November 9, 1914, expressed, as I hope, once and for all, the determined resolve of the British people.

We know to-day even more fully than we did before that there can be no peace in the world until "the military domination of Prussia" is fully and finally destroyed.

I think, however, the British people and their Allies would make one change in Mr Asquith's glowing speech. They would substitute "Germany" for "Prussia." For the blood-guilt of Prussia has infected the entire German nation as with a species of moral leprosy. The German nation as a whole, and not merely the Prussian portion of it, has steeped itself in the vileness of which Prussia, admittedly, was the first and greatest exemplar.

Gone for ever is the theory that we are at war merely with "Prussianism." Our one aim and object to-day must be the utter destruction of the military power of the German Empire as a whole, and the squaring of civilisation's long account with the Germanic peoples. Assuredly until they are brought to see that the courses upon which they have willingly embarked are vile and cruel and wrong—and they can be taught this only by the stern argument of force—the peace of Europe cannot long be preserved. If we falter now, if we and our Allies are content with anything less than overwhelming and decisive victory, it is as certain as the rising of to-morrow's sun that Germany will at once set herself to prepare for a further war of aggression. Nothing but the most decisive humiliation will convince her that the world has no use for men who aim at world-domination. Nothing less will bring home to the minds of her people the clear truth that the megalomaniac dreams of their Emperor have been the sole source of the immeasurable disasters which this War has inflicted upon them.

It is impossible to emphasise too strongly the undeniable truth that for the British Empire this War is and must be decisive. If, in the face of all perils and sacrifices, we persevere to the noble end which Mr Asquith has sketched for us, we can surely see rising in the not very distant future visions of an Empire more glorious even than that of to-day.

In the madness of his dream of world-dominion, the Kaiser fondly believed that one of the first results of the War would be the destruction of the British Empire; he thought that its component parts would fly apart as if by centrifugal force. Never in this world has a rapacious and domineering ruler made a more fatal mistake. The influence of the War upon the constituent elements of the British Empire has been centripetal rather than centrifugal; instead of flying off at a tangent as the Kaiser hoped, our scattered Dominions have drawn in closer and closer still to the tiny island set in the North Sea which, to Britons all the world over, is ever and always "home." War has truly forged new links between us and our brothers overseas, and we may rest content that nothing has contributed more powerfully to the shattering of the Kaiser's dreams than the glorious story of the Anzacs in Gallipoli, the heroism of the Canadians at Ypres, and the devotion with which the dusky sons of India have flung themselves into the world-fray in the cause of the British Raj. Not disruption but unity has sprung from the War. If we preserve that glorious unity to the end, persevering undismayed through the long days that are yet to come of peril and darkness, we shall bequeath to our children and our children's children a heritage which will grow brighter and fairer with the passing of the changing years.

But there must be no faltering in our great resolve, no surrender to weariness or pain, no looking back until our task is done. For us, very literally, *now* is the appointed time. If we fail now, if we put off our harness with our task unfulfilled, if, having set our hand to the plough, we become faint and weak, it needs no strong imagination to see stretching out before us the downward path which must lead the British Empire to disruption and decay.

No matter what the cost, no matter what the sacrifice, we must win this War, and win it so decisively that the menace of Teuton aggression and arrogance, of the immoral doctrine that brute force is the only right, shall be ever removed from civilisation.

Great and glorious are the rewards of success; terrible indeed are the penalties which must await on failure. I implore every single one of my readers to do whatever in him lies to help in the great task of arousing this nation to the fullest possible realisation of the fact that we must either win this War or take our places, humbled and broken, among the nations that no longer count in the councils of the world. For us, at any rate, there is no middle course.

We have to remember that this War will never be settled decisively unless the Allies are able to invade Germany and to inflict a crushing defeat upon the armed force of the enemy. It may be that Germany, faced with certain economic ruin, will sooner or later sue for peace, hoping at least to protect her home territory, to keep her internal resources untouched to be ready for the economic war which will follow the declaration of peace, and to "cut her losses" rather than risk worse things.

Such a peace would be a disaster as great as the War itself, and much greater than the losses involved in its continuance to a decisive ending. It would leave Germany proud in the consciousness that she had faced, not altogether unsuccessfully, an alliance of powerful enemies, and she would simply set to work upon fresh designs of conquest and of preparation for a renewal of the struggle as soon as things looked sufficiently hopeful. And we may be quite sure that Britain, which has had so large a share in the checking of Germany's over-ambitious designs, would be the principal enemy to be aimed at.

Never again could we hope to face Germany upon such favourable terms, and with such powerful Allies. We do not fear the issue of a conflict with Germany single-handed so long as we are warned in time to make our preparations for attack, but we do not want to see the wealth of our Empire and of the other nations wasted in the future in that mad competition of armaments which Germany has forced on the world. Rather would we see the years that are to come years of peace, when the nations shall enjoy a well-earned rest from the burden of militarism which German designs have imposed upon civilisation.

Of all the perils by which we are now threatened, perhaps the very gravest is the conclusion of a premature peace which, in the very nature of things, could be nothing more than a thinly veiled truce to prepare for a new and even more titanic conflict. That is the game which the Germans are playing to-day, and its dangers to us were admirably pointed out by Lord Rosebery in a recent speech. He said:

> There is only one thing which I sometimes fear. It is that when successes begin there may be some weak-minded cry in this

country for a premature peace. A premature peace means a short peace, and a war that will be even worse than this to follow. Therefore let all of us unite in the resolve that while no exertion shall be wanting on our part to bring the War to a triumphant conclusion and the Prussian bloodthirsty tyrants to their knees, yet, on the other hand, not a finger will be raised to accelerate peace before it is justly due.

To that grave and noble warning perhaps I may add the testimony of an officer who is now serving at the front. He writes:

At the present moment there are millions of French, Belgian, Russian, and Serbian peasants wandering about homeless, and there are thousands besides who have died as the result of this wandering about, or who have been actually killed by the Germans as though they had been soldiers in uniform.

Now look at Germany—Germany who will soon be ready for peace! She has hardly had her territory touched; her people do not know what it means to have war waged in their own country.

What I say is that this War must not be finished until it has been carried right into the heart of Germany, so that the German people may know and understand what France, Belgium, Serbia, and Russia have gone through during the last fifteen months.

It is a frightful nightmare to all of us out here that we shall suddenly be told one morning that peace is declared while we are still sitting on this present line of trenches through Belgium and France. No one wants peace more than we do out here, but I—and I know most soldiers are the same—would rather die than see a peace made before we have shown them in Germany what the peasants of the Allies have suffered.

It's no good being soft-hearted with the Germans. I don't think there is any danger of the other Allies being carried away by the premature peace talk; it's only England, who does not know what war means, who may be.

Over and over again the Germans have attempted, with barefaced effrontery, to buy off our Allies, to attempt to induce them to forsake the common cause, to acquiesce, in short, in the betrayal of Britain. That to-day is the keystone of the game of chicanery and fraud which passes in Berlin for diplomacy. There can be no doubt that to France, to Italy, and to Russia splendid gains are freely open as the price of a dishonourable peace; there is to-day hardly any concession which Germany would not willingly make to either of the Allies to secure their withdrawal from the contest.

The one aim of Germany to-day is to detach Britain's Allies, because Germany thinks that with Britain as her sole antagonist she would be sure of ultimate victory. And with her warped code of national honour, with her cynical disregard of the plighted word, she simply cannot understand why the baits she is ready to offer are rejected on all hands with loathing and scorn. She cannot understand the obligations of national honour; she cannot understand that a nation may be too proud to stoop to betrayal for the reward of a bribe. Happily, the bonds which unite the Allies hold firm; and if the Germans cannot see and understand the meaning of the solemn renewal of the Allies' pledge to Belgium, so much the worse for them. Probably they think it is all a piece of bluff, and that we are as ready as they themselves are for peace.

The German gauges every man by his own low standard. He believes that every man has his price; nevertheless, in this belief he exempts the English.

I have before me as I write a copy of recent instructions and advice issued from the German Intelligence Department to its spies. This document is a long and most illuminating one. Here are some quotations from it:

> The officer who has prepared himself by an exhaustive course of technical study cannot fail to acquit himself in intelligence work, *which is more fruitful of distinction than most of the duties of his profession.*
>
> It is rarely advisable to try to conceal one's nationality, but at the same time it is often desirable to assume, especially when in Russia or England, the character and accent of a South German, and to allow it to be understood that he is a member of the Roman Catholic faith.
>
> In England it is well to avoid making any approaches to either a military or naval officer. *They may be regarded as incorruptible.*

The latter sentence of this secret document shows what Germany thinks of our British officers. It shows also to our Allies what our enemies think of us.

The Invisible Hand is ever at work, no doubt. But even the German Intelligence Department, with all its brains and all its cunning, is compelled to admit that we Britons are incorruptible. They have, of course, established the canker-worm in the heart of Great Britain, and we have with us the horde of so-called "naturalised" Germans, so many of whom are impatiently awaiting the downfall of the country to which they have with their traitorous oaths sworn allegiance. But this they have also done in the territory of our Allies, and we may be sure that the scheme which is working tortuously to split the Allies will be persevered in until its futility becomes obvious even to the German mind. It is this plot which explains the peace talk which is beginning to issue so cleverly from Berlin. The design, quite obviously, is either to weaken the solidarity of the Entente or to represent Germany to the neutral nations as the benevolent victor who is ready with the magnanimous offer of the olive-branch as soon as her beaten foes come to their senses.

Such talk may deceive Germans; it may even have some effect upon the very numerous peace body in America with its ludicrous Ford expedition (to whom it is perhaps principally addressed); but it surely can deceive no one else. It does not deceive "the man in the street." We have plenty of evidence that the vast mass of people in the neutral nations realise fully the futility of the German aims, and they are not in the least degree likely to be tempted into proffering peace proposals which would assuredly be instantly rejected by the Allied Powers.

Keen observers among the neutral nations are fully conscious of the fact that Britain's determination to win the War is hardening into that stern and immutable resolve which in all ages has been the dominant characteristic of our people when once their dogged temper was fully aroused. And of the determination of our Allies there is happily not the slightest doubt. They are one and all determined to end once and for all the German menace to the peace of the world.

I believe most firmly that we can win this War if we will. *We have alike the power and the will to win.*

The combined resources of the Allies in men and money are, in the long run, vastly superior to those of Germany and her miserable vassals—for the countries she has dragged into the War with her are, and can be, nothing more. The Central Powers are fighting to-day on four great main fronts, and the drain on their resources is appalling. Germany, in the words of a keen American observer, is being "bled white," and to-day she is striving to secure some vestiges of success to hearten her people, who are beginning to entertain some uneasy doubts as to the reality of the "victories" of which they have heard so much. And her perils are rapidly increasing. Her Turkish Ally has been so badly shaken that we may well look forward to the swift progress of that demoralisation which seems to have already commenced; if Turkey falls by the way, nothing will keep the swelled-headed Bulgarians in the field, and probably nothing would keep the Rumanians and Greeks out of it.

We have to remember that the South-Eastern front is the last chance Germany has of breaking through the iron ring which is ever being drawn tighter and tighter round her throat. Her dreams of expansion eastwards are indeed already shattered, and with the Turkish failure in Armenia probably goes the last hope Germany entertained of being able to call the fight a draw. In the language of the New York *Tribune*, "Germany is now approaching what will be her last great bid for success. But it will not be made on the battlefield; it will be made in conferences, in peace negotiations, and in operations through neutrals." Against that danger it is more than ever necessary for us to be on our guard.

And that danger is undoubtedly increased by the mischievous and traitorous chatter of the peace cranks who in our own country are slowly recovering their courage, and are beginning to make their noisy voices heard. These are the people who at the moment are the real enemies of our country, the real pro-Germans. They are not very numerous, but they are very noisy; they are not very intelligent, but they are very persistent; and, like all "martyrs," so-called, they are imbued with the firm conviction that they alone are right, and that all the rest of our people are wrong. They are industrious with the industry of the true fanatic, and they are striving by every means in their power, fair or foul, to swing the wavering and the faint-hearted to their cause.

Already the croaking voice of the peace crank has been heard even in the House of Lords itself, and it might have been heard still more loudly if the public, with a just perception of the mischief these pestilent people are doing, had not taken more than once rough-and-ready measures to put a stop to their misguided energies.

I am no advocate of mob law, but if the peace advocates persist in turning the principle of free speech into a licence for a traitorous propaganda I confess I cannot sympathise deeply with their shrieks for sympathy when an indignant public turns upon them in the only way open to it, and refuses to allow their voices to be heard.

That the heart of the people is sound upon this question of fighting the War to the only conclusion compatible with our national honour and safety I am to-day firmly convinced.

Yet there is a very real risk that the cry of "Stop the War!" may make too many converts among the unthinking sections who, like all of us, are weary of the War and long to see peace restored. None of us desires to see the War prolonged, with all its terrible cost in blood and treasure; but, on the other hand, no Englishman worthy the name can fail to share the view expressed by Lord Rosebery. It is the business of all loyal Britons to see that the poisonous propaganda which finds its best representation in such egregious bodies as the "Union of Democratic Control" shall be decisively countered. It is the business of the nation to concentrate all its energies to-day upon the winning of a clear and unmistakable victory which shall ensure the peace of Europe for a century to come.

It is a very striking characteristic of Germany that the better things are going the more loudly she talks of the great things she is going to do in the immediate future. Every trifling success she wins produces an outburst of extravagant boasting wholly disproportionate to the achievement. In the early days of the War, what the Germans call, with their usual lack of good taste, the "big mouth" (*grosse Schnautze*) was very much in evidence. It has cooled down very considerably of late, and its place is being taken by a very much more chastened frame of mind.

The olive-branch is much in evidence, and the mailed fist is somewhat at a discount. "Frightfulness" is, in the main, left to the sabre-rattling Count Reventlow, the puff-ball Captain Persius, and to that portion of the German Press which takes its leading articles direct from the Government lie-factory in Berlin. Ananias has his hand heavily over Germany at the present moment. Otherwise the tone is one of a benignant willingness to admit that Germany and all the other countries have been very much to blame, and that it is time this terrible War was ended. This new species of modesty by compulsion is all a part of the German dodge to try to make a favourable peace which would leave Germany weakened indeed—it is realised that that can hardly be avoided—but by no means whipped. It is our business to stick to our task until the whipping is obvious not only to the whole world, but to the German people as well.

The times are full of perils, yet they are not without hope. Already we see the rifts in the dark clouds which have hung over us for so long. And if we turn a deaf ear to those who counsel the way of ignominious ease, if we decide to persevere with all our heart and all our strength along the path of noble purpose upon which we have embarked, we shall reach in good time to the long-desired haven of victory and peace and prosperity.

I defined in this hall exactly a year ago the objects without the attainment of which the Allies will not lay down their arms. They remain to-day as they were then. We pursue them one and all with undiminished faith; we believe that we have advanced a long way to their achievement. Be the journey long or short we shall not falter till we have secured for the smaller states of Europe their charter of Independence, and for Europe itself and for the world at large its final emancipation from the reign of force.—*Mr Asquith, at The Guildhall, November 9, 1915.*

Chapter Twelve
"Never Again"

It would be nothing less than a crime against civilisation if, after the War has come to a close, Germany is left with the power again to make herself a menace to the peace of our modern civilised world.

We need have no sentimental considerations on this point. We want none. Germany has shown conclusively that she is not to be bound by any considerations of honour, and that she has deliberately aimed at what the world will never tolerate—world-dominion in the hands of a single Power. We and our Allies have determined that she shall not be allowed to realise her ambitions in this direction; it is our duty to see that for the future, in the interests of humanity as a whole, she is robbed of the power of making herself a nuisance and a danger to her neighbours, who wish only to live in peace.

If peace for the moment were the only object of the Allies, their wishes could be gratified on very easy terms.

There is no doubt whatever that Germany would be glad to bring the War to a close before she is more seriously weakened, if not utterly ruined; it is our business and the business of our Allies to see that no premature peace is allowed to rob them of the fruits of their great sacrifices. For, be it remembered, their real object is not so much victory now, except inasmuch as victory will enable them to gain security in the future. We do not want a world kept perpetually on tenterhooks by Germany's exhibitions of the "mailed fist"; and unless I misread entirely the signs of the times, I do not think we are likely to have it. Germany will have to be dealt with after the War, and no feelings of pity or consideration for a defeated enemy can have any influence on the settlement.

For years past Germany has deliberately elected to make economic war in times of peace. Of this we have no reason to complain; a country's fiscal arrangements are a matter for itself. But out of her economic war Germany grew rich and strong enough to wage military war, and she will do so again unless we and our Allies take steps to stop her. Now in this matter old shibboleths have got to go by the board, and there is every indication that, not as a matter of politics, but as a mere matter of self-preservation, both Britain and the Allies are preparing to fight Germany in the future with the weapon which in the past has proved so successful against themselves.

There are very few things indeed produced by Germany which Britain or her Allies cannot produce for themselves, and I have no hesitation in saying that for the future our fiscal watchword ought to be, "The Allies first and the rest nowhere." I do not want to see this or that party snatch a party advantage out of our old quarrels on the subject of Free Trade.

I have every hope that as a result of the War many of our old suicidal party divisions and petty bickerings will disappear, never to return; and for this reason I hope—perhaps it is hoping against hope—that when the War is over we shall consider our future tariff system not as Liberals or Conservatives, but as Imperialists pure and simple.

It is true, speaking broadly, that the Liberal Party as a whole is so deeply pledged to Free Trade that any reversal of its policy on this subject must be a matter of grave difficulty. But the question is no longer Free Trade or Tariff Reform; the question to-day is, or at least in the near future will be, the maintenance of Britain's commercial prosperity against German attacks which are sure to be renewed the instant peace is declared.

There are those who think—the wish is father to the thought—that Germans will be so unpopular after the War that there will be no risk of their doing business in any British territory, and that many of the neutrals even will refuse to have dealings with them. I think it is undoubtedly true that in many cases and in many countries Germans will find that they are not received in the future as they have been in the past. But the Fownes case shows us very clearly that there are Englishmen who are not averse to trading with Germany even in time of War when such trading is expressly forbidden. What reason have we, then, to think that after peace is declared there will not be found hundreds of firms quite ready to trade with Germans if by so doing they can make a profit? And if this is true of England, can we blame the neutral nations and our Allies if they are no more scrupulous?

Our policy must be to make such trading impossible because unprofitable—firstly, to encourage our own business men throughout the Empire and the business men belonging to the nations that are allied with us, and, secondly, to prevent Germany gaining in the commercial world a position which will enable her again to grow so rich and so strong that she will be enabled in her own time again to menace our security.

There is only one way to secure that end, and that is by a preferential tariff which shall operate in all the Allied countries in favour of Allied goods. At whatever cost in the sacrifice of long-held political convictions, some such measure is imperative if we are not to be faced with the prospect of another and more terrible war just as soon as Germany feels herself strong enough to wage it.

Now it is very significant and very important that at least two Ministers whose Free Trade proclivities cannot be suspected have warned the country that in the future we shall see great alterations in our fiscal policy. Mr Runciman and Mr Montagu have given expression to very similar views, and perhaps I may quote a few words from the speech which the latter made at Cambridge, when he said there were two topics of enormous importance that every man, Liberal or Conservative, would have to keep an open mind upon under the new conditions.

> The first (he proceeded) is the fiscal system. It cannot have escaped notice that in the House of Commons last year Liberal Free Traders and Conservative Tariff Reformers, leaders of both parties, expressed their opinions that the old economic condition of the relationship between the different parts of the globe would be altered after the War, and without saying to-day what the answer will be to those problems I will say that it is not a part of Liberalism not to recognise altered conditions and circumstances, and to revise or perhaps strengthen ourselves in respect to the new conditions which may arise. We in the past conducted trade as a peaceful pursuit, and treated all nations as nearly as we could equally. But look at the history of this War and see the use Germany made of her trade, and just ask yourselves whether we can ever afford or dare to let that happen again.

Now, when he made that speech Mr Montagu was speaking to an assemblage of Liberals, and it is not without significance that his remarks were received with loud cheers. There is, indeed, no doubt whatever that Liberals and Conservatives are rapidly drawing nearer together on this great question, and the outlook for a solution along truly Imperial lines is brighter than it has been for many years past. So great are the changes which have been produced by Germany's mad ambition and greed!

Even Manchester, the home of Free Trade orthodoxy, has revolted against the idea that there shall be free trade with Germany after the War.

The Chamber of Commerce of that city has by an overwhelming majority declared itself opposed to anything of the kind. In London a great meeting of business men at the Guildhall, presided over by the Lord Mayor, has called emphatically for a policy which shall smash for ever the German commercial-military system, shall formulate action for the defence and improvement of trade after the War, and shall improve our commercial relations with the Overseas Dominions and the Allies. A strong subcommittee of the Board of Trade has reported emphatically in favour of preference for our Allies and in favour of tariff protection for all industries which are of national necessity. And the committee adds, very significantly, "In view of the threatened dumping of stocks which may be accumulated in enemy countries, the Government should take such steps as would prevent the position of industries likely to be affected being endangered after the War or during the period required for a wider consideration of the whole question."

This can be done, in the committee's opinion, by import duties which, directed against German and enemy products, would go far to shut them out of the British Empire. The committee even goes so far as to recommend that certain goods coming from enemy countries shall be absolutely refused admission.

We have shown ourselves in the past very far behind the Overseas Dominions in our willingness to advance the cause of British trade for British traders. We must do so no longer. The enormous contributions the Dominions have made to the Empire's cause imperatively demand that in the future their devotion shall be recognised, and one of the subjects upon which they feel most keenly is that we do not at present do enough to encourage their young but rapidly growing industries.

If we adopt the policy of "Empire goods for the Empire," we shall draw still closer the bonds which unite old England to her younger sons. And surely, putting our own self-interest aside, our gallant Allies have some reason to look to Britain for help in fighting the German octopus. They as well as we are vitally interested in making peace secure after this terrible struggle; and just as the War has been in the main brought about by Germany's economic expansion being turned to evil purposes, so peace will be secured only by her being prevented from waging economic war in the future. And the best way to secure that end is to establish in the British Empire and all the Allied nations a tariff wall that shall amount to a virtual boycott of German products of every kind whatever. There will be no reluctance on the part of our Allies to join us in such a policy; Russia, indeed, has already announced that her trade is closed to Germany for all time.

There is another reason why such a boycott should appeal specially to England. During this War we have made advances amounting to many hundreds of millions to the Allies who are fighting with us in the cause of civilisation. That money will sooner or later be repaid, and on every account it will be best repaid in the way of trade. The more closely we can, after the War, confine our foreign trade to our Allies, the more easily and the more quickly will they be able to reduce their indebtedness to us. A lasting commercial compact between the Allied Powers will not only be a powerful financial help to all of them, but it will be perhaps the most powerful instrument that could be devised for preserving the peace of the world.

We have seen during the past few years what the Germans meant and have done by the methods of "peaceful penetration." Unless some remedy is devised those methods will be put into operation again directly after the War. Antwerp is a standing case in point. Belgians and French alike denounced the insidious plot to make of Antwerp a purely German port; but although ninety per cent, of the trade was handled and owned by Germans, and brought no profit to Belgium, the scandal—for it was nothing less—was allowed to continue. In England, especially in London, and in our Dominions we have seen the same evil. The case of the Merton firm, some of whose associates had secured practically the monopoly of the world's trade in base metals, gives us an object-lesson which I trust we shall not forget. London traders can tell strange stories of "peaceful penetration" of British industries. They know how countless German clerks came over to work at low wages "just to learn the language." They found out too late that these clerks all received a subsidy from the German Government, that they were really German commercial spies in the pay of rival firms, and that any employer who admitted these aliens into his establishment was sure soon to note a falling-off in orders, due to the alien clerks having access to confidential correspondence and advising their paymasters in Germany accordingly. And those self-same clerks received from Germany a premium if they married English girls! Now no tariff will furnish absolute protection against such methods as this; the British trader will have himself to thank if he is caught again by the same device. But we have to remember that the Hun is amazingly ingenious in every description of underhand work, and that fresh plans will be devised if the old ones fail. We must take measures accordingly. And one of those measures must be a stringent revision of the law relating to naturalisation. We want no more Germans naturalised in this country for many a long year to come.

We want no more Germans over here acting as spies in either the military or the commercial field. We will tolerate none. Further, I hope that after the War is over we shall see an effective passport system introduced which shall apply to all foreigners, and that before any German or Austrian is allowed even to reside in the country he will be compelled to obtain some kind of guarantee of good behaviour from some responsible English firm.

Only by some such means can we make it difficult or impossible for the worst class of our enemies to swarm over here directly peace is signed.

Coupled with efficient passport restrictions, I hope to see an effective check put upon the admission of undesirable aliens of any and every nation. We do not want a lot of foreign wastrels whose countries are only too glad to be rid of them swarming into England to flood the already overcrowded labour market and, willing to live in hopeless penury, bringing down the price of wages here to the detriment of our own people. Something has been done of late years to reduce this scandal; I hope still more will be done in the future.

Then we have the question of German-controlled firms operating under English names and with English registration. This system must absolutely stop. Whether it will be possible for German firms openly to trade here after the War I do not know, but at any rate we must have no more Teutons posing as British, and Huns acquiring control of British industries. The name "German" shall be an everlasting stigma. The powers which the Government now possess to control any firm shown to be of enemy nationality should be continued, and there ought to be devised some means of putting an end to the scandals which for years past have given the Germans unrivalled opportunities for worming their way into the English commercial world.

I have no doubt whatever that many reputable British firms will in the future hesitate very considerably before they do any business with Germany. But we have to recognise that there are others who will be less scrupulous, and who will reck nothing of the danger to the country if they see the chance of turning a more or less honest penny. Those are the people against whom, in the interests of our Empire, we have to be on our guard.

We have ample evidence that the awakening of the British commercial community to the dangers which will threaten it immediately after peace is declared has aroused the utmost consternation and resentment in Germany. That is at once its best justification and its strongest recommendation. The Germans have openly boasted, both before and since war broke out, that British firms could not do business without certain goods from Germany. The fact that we have done so for the past eighteen months is sufficient answer, and it is enough to show that we can do so in the future.

It is true, of course, that we had, weakly enough, allowed ourselves to become dependent upon Germany for scores of German-made articles. Such vital necessities as chemicals of various kinds and the aniline dyes are good instances. Even now we are suffering from the lack of some of them. But there is no mistaking the fact that we are very rapidly finding substitutes for what we formerly imported from Germany. The making of

British dyes, for example, is progressing by leaps and bounds; and there is no doubt that if our traders are given half the encouragement that is given to German traders by the German Government, they will very soon show that they have nothing to learn from their German rivals. Every day we get new evidence that British firms are more and more completely adapting themselves to the altered conditions, and laying down extensive plant for the manufacture of just those articles we used to purchase dearly from our Teutonic competitors. That policy must be ours for all time.

What Germans have done we can do. The German is great at imitating and improving, but he has little originality; he is like the Japanese, quick to see a good thing and adapt it, but not so quick to invent. We have to see for the future that we are as quick as he is to adapt and a great deal quicker to invent, and unless we do so we shall in a very few years' time see arise in a new form many of the troubles which, if we handle the commercial position aright, ought never again to disturb us.

"Never again" must be our watchword in dealing with the accursed German competition. Our people must be educated to a permanent boycott of German goods; if they will not learn, they must be compelled. Our manufacturers must be protected against the policy of dumping bounty-fed goods throughout our Empire at rates with which it is impossible for them to compete because the German Government makes it possible for the German trader to sell even below cost price with the object of ousting his British rival. Socially and commercially we must be protected against the flood of aliens who have already done untold harm to British labour. All this we have done for eighteen months; we must do it in perpetuity for the future.

But when all is said and done we cannot make our position in the world secure unless our trading classes are prepared to revise very considerably many of the methods they have adopted for years past. The time when British goods sold merely because they were British, and therefore the best on the market, has gone for ever. To-day commercial competition is keen beyond anything of which our forefathers had knowledge, and our methods unfortunately have not kept pace with the changing circumstances.

There has been too much of the old happy-go-lucky style about us; we have been too much inclined to rest upon our reputation, and to think that because all was well fifty or a hundred years ago, all must be well to-day.

The sooner that idea disappears from the minds of our business men the better it will be for them and for the Empire. Never was the King's message, "Wake up, England," more urgently necessary than it is to-day. Proper measures taken by our Government will make it easier for us to beat the Germans in the future in the field of commerce. But no measures which Governments can take will wholly replace business ability and energy. Just as, given proper weapons, our soldiers can beat the Germans in the field of war, so we can beat the Germans in the field of commerce if our commercial soldiers are given weapons adequate to the task they have in hand. But neither the weapons of war nor the weapons of commerce will avail us *unless they are used by men with clear heads, strong hearts, and unbounded energy and determination.*

As this volume goes to press the Titanic struggle for Verdun—the battle which may well decide the War—rages with undiminished fury. What the outcome may be none can say, but, at least, the omens are good. After over a fortnight of furious fighting, after the expenditure of many lives and enormous quantities of ammunition, the Huns have utterly failed to pierce the French defence. The troops of France are fighting like heroes: her generals are serene and confident. Germany has staked her all on this gigantic thrust. Failure would spell national depression on an unparalleled scale, and add to the German Government's growing difficulties. And if Verdun falls, will the victory be worth the price? We know that almost any position can be taken if losses are disregarded. But whether Verdun will ever be worth to the Germans the price they will have to pay for its capture is, to say the least of it, exceedingly doubtful. But the Germans are deeply committed to the venture, and it may be that they will consider no price too high to pay—for they hold "cannon-fodder" cheap—in order to save what remains of their badly shattered national, military, and dynastic prestige.